A Devotional Experience Of the Gospel

JONATHAN CASHMAN

WITH ANDREW SARGENT PH.D.

To my mom, whose strength and courage
never ceased to amaze me.
Thank you for showing me what unconditional love and support
looks like.
I love you.

WE WANT TO HEAR FROM YOU!

You can post any of your comments or questions by joining in the conversation on the forum page at www.saviorgroups.com

For more information about the SAVIOR Musical, behind the scenes video footage, live events, or information on Jonathan Cashman, go to www.SAVIORmusical.com, *or* www.thecashmans.org

You can follow both Jonathan and Dr. Sargent on Facebook at SAVIOR MUSICAL or Biblical Literacy Ministries. You can also follow Dr. Sargent on twitter @DrAndrewSargent and join his forum at www.DrAndrewSargent.com

Britney Cashman's worship music is available at www.britneycashman.com

Like us on Facebook under Savior Musical & The Cashmans, *or* Biblical Literacy Ministries.

For booking information go to www.BLMinistries.net, *or* www.SAVIORmusical.com, www.TheCashmans.org, *or* email: booking@saviormusical.com *or* cashmanministries@gmail.com

Unless otherwise noted, all Scripture quotations are from the NKJ

TABLE OF CONTENTS

FORWARD

We know that vision attracts people to a ministry, but relationships give it value. I've had the privilege of working with Jonathan Cashman long enough to know he has a passion for worship and the spiritual formation of people. Jonathan and I developed somewhat of a father/son relationship during our ministry time together at Calvary Assembly in Orlando, FL. Though SAVIOR is more than a decade long endeavor for Jonathan and his wife, Britney, my first introduction to SAVIOR was while Jonathan was serving as the Worship and Life Group Pastor at Calvary. It is a joy to write the foreword for 40 Days with the SAVIOR and to see another one of his dreams fulfilled. These forty devotionals will not only give you rewarding insights into the gospel, but will also reveal the heart and soul of Jonathan for his SAVIOR. They are practical and engaging; they will make a positive difference as you meditate on them.

I highly recommend these inspiring devotional stories. Though a blessing year round, SAVIOR works as a great small group program in the 40-days leading from Ash Wednesday to Easter. There's no time like the present to use them for any individual or group. You will want to come back to them again and again.

Bob Rhoden, D.Min.
Author of FOUR FACES OF A LEADER

INTRODUCTION

Welcome to the start of your 40 day spiritual journey! This devotional is designed to help you experience Jesus the SAVIOR as you walk with him through the last week of his earthly ministry. You will get a disciple's point of view as you watch each scene unfold. Along the way, you will meet the characters and contemplate many important connections between your own struggles and theirs.

This 40 day devotional was originally written to engage each passage of the gospels that inspired the 40 songs of the SAVIOR Musical. The devotional can stand alone, but the songs of SAVIOR help to aid in the experience, capturing the moods and emotions of each event. Within various devotions, you'll get a little behind the scenes glimpse both of the spiritual journey of the main author and the creation and development of the musical.

This devotional is meant to be interactive. Each chapter comes with penetrating application questions intended to help you passionately and meaningfully engage its content as it relates to your own past, present, and hoped for future. The depth of your experience with the SAVIOR through these devotions will largely depend on your willingness to participate in the discussion with open and contemplative responses to these questions. The chapters are short, but we highly recommend that you limit yourself to one per day. If you miss a day, don't get discouraged, just jump back in.

We also highly recommend that you find someone to share the journey with you as either a devotional partner, or as part of a discussion group. This will not only help you maintain the discipline needed to remain committed to what can be a deep and challenging spiritual growth process, but will also give you an opportunity to share in other people's insights, people whose own unique experiences may complement your own. If you let it, the next 40 days can transform your life.

May the Lord guide you on your journey!

Jonathan Cashman & Andrew Sargent

1

 ## IT BEGINS

Isaiah 52:13-53:6

Behold, My Servant shall deal prudently; He shall be exalted and extolled and be very high. Just as many were astonished at you, so His visage was marred more than any man, and His form more than the sons of men; so shall He sprinkle many nations. Kings shall shut their mouths at Him; for what had not been told them they shall see, and what they had not heard they shall consider.

Who has believed our report? And to whom has the arm of the Lord been revealed? For he comes up before him as a tender plant, and as a root out of a dry ground; he has no form nor majesty that we should see him, nor an appearance that we should desire him. He was despised and rejected of men, a man of sorrows, familiar with suffering. Like one from whom men hide their faces; he was despised, and we esteemed him not.

Surely he took up our infirmities and carried our sorrows; yet we considered him stricken by God, smitten by him, and afflicted. But he was pierced for our transgressions, he was crushed for our iniquities. The punishment that brought us peace was upon him, and by his stripes we are healed. We all like sheep have gone astray; each of us has turned to our own way; and the Lord has laid on him the iniquity of us all.

SAVIOR?

Welcome to the first of forty days with the SAVIOR.

To use the term SAVIOR, referring to God as the SAVIOR of mankind, suggests obviously that humanity needs saving. It implies that there is some problem so threatening to our existence, our eternal existence, a danger so beyond our own capacity to escape, that it demands divine deliverance. The prophet Isaiah describes just such a problem and anticipates God stepping in, sending his "Servant" to deliver humanity from eternal danger.

Regardless of where your personal beliefs lie, Jesus of Nazareth, whom the gospels declare to be this very Servant, the hero of our devotional, is the most significant person in human history. No one has shaped the world more than Jesus... and nothing can match the impact that the Scriptures, which reveal him, have had on the world.

Just so, when it came time to write the opening of the SAVIOR Musical, one of the last pieces added, I could not think of a more significant place to begin the story of this incredible figure than with what I consider the most powerful prophecy about him, the prophecy that reveals his nature as SAVIOR most clearly. 750 years before Jesus was born into the world, the prophet Isaiah anticipated the coming of Christ and revealed the inconceivable truth about his work in mind blowing terms. Whether a person believes, or does not believe, these are matters not to be taken lightly, or ignored.

BELIEF

I struggled with issues of belief into my early adult life. Even though I attended Catholic school from 4th grade to the 9th grade, I didn't understand the gospel at all. For example, a friend of mine once told me that if I opened the Bible and read the book of Revelation three times in a row that I would go to heaven... so I did. The book made zero sense to me. All of the descriptions of multi-headed monsters, weird looking animals, beasts, angels and dragons just confused me. My lack of understanding of what it meant to believe, however, gave me a false sense of confidence in my eternal destiny.

In my early twenties, I was in a band called, *The Trees*. We had just finished an album, and our minor record label was showcasing us to some of the major labels—*Yay!* Things seemed to be going according to our plans when our guitarist, David, who'd been playing with us since high school, "gave his life to Jesus Christ," as he described his new found religious devotion. He was just your average Dave one day, then, suddenly, devout… so devout that I thought he might quit the band. Thankfully he didn't.

After practice one night, we all sat around and talked. Dave told us about his new relationship with Christ and was riddled with cynical questions from the guys in the band. I admired his tenacity. He'd always been a meek and soft-spoken guy, but, that night, he had a joyful confidence and an impressive determination. David and his wife, Shelby, knew what they would be in for by carrying on a conversation about Jesus with us. He knew we would think they had gone overboard. They had remained humble, however, and politely listened, doing their best to answer each question as they told us how Christ had changed their hearts.

As stated, I attended Catholic schools and went to church as a kid, so, at some point in the conversation, I turned to Shelby and said, "I believe in God." I wanted to let her know that I was on her side, but, rather than getting an "atta-boy," or the "oh-that's-great" that I was expecting, she paused, looked me in the eye and asked, "Where is the fruit of that?"

The strange question caught me off guard, but even through her Christianized language, I understood what she meant—*How did my statement of belief translate into my life?* Her question caused me to think about what believing actually meant. I could say that I believed in "God," in theory, but I really couldn't say that I believed his message, "his report," because first, I didn't understand the gospel of Jesus Christ, and second, my lifestyle couldn't back up my claims of belief. Frankly, I lived as if there were no God.

THE SERVANT DRAMA

The prophet Isaiah was familiar with struggles like mine. He knew all about belief and unbelief. His prophecy is a little bit of a skit where the prophet plays all the parts. The prophet plays the role of God, announcing how his Servant would come to suffer and die to redeem mankind from their sins. This, however, sounds nuts even to the prophet who next plays himself in the drama. He asks the most pertinent question. Imagine him throwing up his hands in disgust and shouting, "Yeah, that's awesome, but who will believe it?"

If you believe this gospel message already, it might make some kind of sense to you. Jesus came as God in human form to die for the sins of the whole world... naturally! If you do not believe, however, I am not insensible to how crazy this may sound. Isaiah knew it sounded crazy, that's for sure; that's why he asked that all-important question; "Who has believed our report? And to whom has the arm of the Lord been revealed?" The answer you give to this question in your own heart will be one of the most defining things about you.

HELP MY UNBELIEF

No matter how great Jesus is, no matter how important the Bible has been for human history, believing is not merely about acknowledging historical facts. People show what they believe by what they do, by the choices they make. A "believer" isn't defined by a once upon a time profession, but by an ongoing commitment to "truths" lived out. Belief in Christ can start small, but it starts with a practical commitment to the person and teachings of Jesus, who he says he is, what he says he's done, and what he asks of us. Belief can be hard; it is a life-long process. Indeed, I think anyone who knows a little of their own heart, can echo the words of the man who said to Christ, "Lord, I believe; help my unbelief!"

As you journey through this devotional, our desire is that you consider what you believe and how your beliefs translate into your life. We hope you come to understand more of who Jesus is, his gospel message and the purpose that he's planned for you. We pray that your beliefs are strengthened and applied, that they transform your life into the image and plan that God has intended.

LIFE APPLICATIONS:

1. Describe your beliefs about Jesus. Describe the gospel in your own words.

_____

_____

_____

_____

_____

_____

_____

_____

_____

_____

2. Explain what you think is meant by the statement, "Lord, I believe; help my unbelief!" Can you relate? Which of the things that you profess to believe are the hardest for you to live out?

_____

_____

_____

_____

_____

_____

_____

_____

_____

_____

2

HOSANNA

Matthew 21:1-11

Now when they drew near Jerusalem, and came to Bethphage, at the Mount of Olives, then Jesus sent two disciples, saying to them, "Go into the village opposite you, and immediately you will find a donkey tied, and a colt with her. Loose them and bring them to me. And if anyone says anything to you, you shall say, 'The Lord has need of them,' and immediately he will send them."

All this was done that it might be fulfilled which was spoken by the prophet, saying, "Tell the daughter of Zion, 'Behold, your king is coming to you, lowly, and sitting on a donkey, a colt, the foal of a donkey.'" So the disciples went and did as Jesus commanded them. They brought the donkey and the colt, laid their clothes on them, and set him on them.

And a very great multitude spread their clothes on the road; others cut down branches from the trees and spread them on the road. Then, the multitudes who went before and those who followed cried out, saying:

"Hosanna to the son of David! 'Blessed is he who comes in the name of the Lord!' Hosanna in the highest!"

And when he had come into Jerusalem, all the city was moved, saying, "Who is this?" So the multitudes said, "This is Jesus…"

THE LORD HAS NEED OF HIM

As I read this passage, I can't get my mind off this donkey. Odd, I know. We have this great moment of messianic fervor in the streets of Jerusalem, with the masses breaking out in song, perhaps, akin to a Christmas mall flash mob, but I'm thinking about the donkey. Maybe it's because, in this donkey, tied and bound, but called for a purpose, I see myself and my own encounter with Christ many years ago.

THE TREES

After David, the guitarist in my band, The Trees, came to Christ, his one condition for staying in the band was that we would have to add two Christian songs to our repertoire—*Groan.*

So Dave and his wife, Shelby, showed up for rehearsal in my basement one night with a beat-up double-deck tape player with a shoestring for a handle. When we finished rehearsing our set list, Dave announced that it was time for us to learn our new Christian songs from the shoestring jukebox. Eyes rolled; stomachs turned.

I went over to the tape deck and fast-forwarded through a few songs, playing bits of each; they were old bluegrass tunes with titles like- *I Like the Christian Life* and *I Am a Pilgrim.* I was less than impressed; my eyes pleaded, "Dave, do you have anything else?" Nothing. Bluegrass is fine, but these songs had lyrics like, yonder, garment hem, heeding, and wearisome; besides, we played rock. The band reluctantly agreed to play only *one* of the songs from the tape deck for the next night's show.

I AM A PILGRIM

That Saturday night, at the Massachusetts Blackstone Bar and Grille, we played our own rock version of *I Am a Pilgrim.* After the show, we came back and partied at my house with a bunch of our friends. Dave and I had been talking a lot about the Lord and God's will for our lives. I was becoming more fascinated with the things of God; I agreed to go to church with him the next day.

The following morning, he picked me up and we went to his

small, white, classic New England church called *Grace Chapel*. I found it interesting that, living less than a mile from the place, on the same street, I had hardly noticed that it was there. We walked into the 100 seat sanctuary, and an exuberantly happy gentleman greeted us at the door. A band was playing Christian church music up front, and we sat down towards the back.

As we sat, listening to the band, something amazingly strange started happening to me; I sensed the presence of God and started to cry. To this day, I don't remember what was preached, or what songs were sung, but I do remember crying... a lot. All I could do was sit in my seat with my head down on my arm, soaking the sleeve of my tweed jacket, as a strong sense of the love, power and purity of the Spirit of God overwhelmed me.

I remember thinking, *Ok, Jonathan, stop crying*, but I couldn't. The loving presence of the Holy Spirit was too strong. It was as if he was scrubbing me clean, breaking the bonds of sin, setting me free. He was healing my heart and filling me. I had the strongest impression that the Lord was calling me to do something for him. It was as if he was saying to me, "You will write songs for *me* now." It was a humbling experience. I was unqualified, unable, and I knew it.

I was that donkey. David and Shelby had been sent for me. They told me later that they knew the Lord was calling out someone in our band, but they didn't know which one of us it was at the time.

When the disciples went, Jesus told them that if anyone asks why they are taking the donkey, they are to tell them, "The Lord has need of him." We might paraphrase, "The Lord has a purpose for him."

And what was this purpose? The greatest honor that could be bestowed upon a donkey. He carried the Lord into Jerusalem in triumphal entry, bringing the SAVIOR to his people, where he is heralded and honored as the long awaited Messiah.

They cried out, saying: 'Hosanna to the son of David!' 'Blessed is he who comes in the name of the LORD!' 'Hosanna in the highest!' Jesus comes to them with the donkey's help, fulfilling centuries old prophecies of the Messiah's arrival. Zechariah 9:9 predicts, "Rejoice greatly, O daughter of Zion! Shout, O daughter of Jerusalem! Behold, your king is coming to you; he is just and having salvation, lowly and riding on a donkey, a colt, the foal of a donkey."

Before the donkey could fulfill his majestic purpose for the Lord, however, he needed to be sought out, freed from his bonds and brought to Christ. He needed to yield himself to Jesus. That day in that small New England church, I yielded my life to Christ.

LIFE APPLICATIONS:

1. As the colt was tied and bound, what are some things that have or had you bound, keeping you from fulfilling the will of God in your life? If there has been a time in your life that you felt that God freed you from something to serve him, please describe it.

_____

_____

_____

_____

_____

_____

_____

_____

_____

_____

2. Do you believe that the Lord has some plan for your life? If so, explain it.

_____

_____

_____

_____

_____

_____

_____

_____

_____

3. The disciples loosed the donkey for the Lord's purpose. Have you ever served this function in someone else's life? What was the outcome? Is there someone in your life now whom the Lord is calling you to help set free, to bring to him? What are you doing about it?

_____

_____

_____

_____

_____

_____

_____

_____

_____

_____

_____

𝟹

IF YOU ONLY KNEW

Luke 19:41-44

As *Jesus* drew near, he saw the city and wept over it, saying, "If you had known, even you, especially in this your day, the things that make for your peace! But now they are hidden from your eyes. For days will come upon you when your enemies will build an embankment around you, surround you and close you in on every side, and level you, and your children within you, to the ground; and they will not leave in you one stone upon another, because you did not know the time of your visitation."

PRECONCIEVED NOTIONS

God often gives you what you need in a package you don't want. Many of the Jews awaiting the Messiah in Jesus' day were looking for a conquering king who would free them from the Romans, who then occupied Israel. They believed what the Scriptures taught—that a messiah would be coming—but pictured him in terms of an earthly ruler of an earthly kingdom. He came, instead, as a priestly king of a heavenly kingdom. They knew that Messiah would be a SAVIOR, but only envisioned him as a SAVIOR bringing them what they wanted—salvation from Roman bondage and oppression. Jesus came, instead, as SAVIOR from the bondage of sin and the oppression of Satan's occupation. The thing that they needed most in all the world came walking among them, and they missed it.

I can relate to those who missed the Lord when he came. I can relate to their misconstrued notions regarding Christ; I've had many of my own. The fact is, it's easier for us to believe in a god of our own imagination, than the God revealed in Scripture. Even when we read the Scriptures, we can easily be selective in the texts that we allow to inform our vision of God, our understanding of his character, his attributes, his plan for our lives.

It's not hard to craft an image of God that suits us and our lifestyle; one that makes us feel safe, in control, guaranteed to get from life the things we want most. Some envision God as The Big Santa Claus in the sky, spending most of their lives just trying to stay off the naughty list. Who wouldn't love the idea of an all-powerful Santa-god, dedicated to giving us what we want most in this life? That is so much more appealing than a God who has his own agenda, than a God who tells us what to do, and worse, yet, what *not* to do.

God has revealed himself, his character, his purpose, in the pages of Scripture. Therefore, crafting unbiblical images of God in our minds is little different than carving and worshiping gods of wood and stone. These mental idols, these idols of the heart, are what lay at the bottom of the rejection of Jesus. He, who was the very character and nature of God in human form, was unrecognizable to them, and they missed their day of visitation. Jesus offered them, "The things that made for (their) peace," a path to peace with God, their rejection of Jesus brought only the promise of desolation.

THE DAY OF THE LORD'S VISITATION

The Lord visited me in a time in my life when I had things going the way that I wanted them. I was in a rock band and had spent about five years writing and developing songs with my writing partner, Rich. I played the guitar, and he played bass, and we both sang. Our band had quite a repertoire developing when Dave and I came to Christ. We spent two years recording our album, and our small record label was, as I've mentioned, showcasing us to bigger record companies. It all seemed to be happening, but, after I committed my life to Christ, it just didn't feel right anymore.

I tried to carry on as usual in the band, but the Lord was drawing me out of it. I'd be lying if I told you that I wanted to leave the band; I didn't. I wanted to continue doing what we were doing; it was my lifelong dream. God had other plans, however, and I fought against those plans for some time. As Jesus said when he entered Jerusalem, I didn't realize what *made for* my peace and I could've missed my day of his visitation—that great moment of divine opportunity.

In those early days, I was at Dave and Shelby's place almost every night, studying the Bible with them. I would abrade them with endless questions and concerns, and they did their best to guide and disciple me. My biggest struggle was with music, mainly our music. Our band and our songs were a large part of my life, and I didn't want that to change. I knew God was calling me to write music for him, but that was a drastic contrast to my own musical plans. Throughout those nights at Dave and Shelby's, they never told me that I had to stop playing or writing my own non-Christian music, but that didn't help my anxiety. In fact, what was bothering me the most was that nobody was telling me I had to stop, except my heart; that was where the struggle was. God was changing me.

I became more verbal about my struggle and soon formed an argument that I would give to every spiritual advisor in my life. I could've entitled it: *Why I Don't Have to Write Christian Music.* I gave this argument to my pastor, other pastors, elders at the church and to anyone who would listen (*…and you see that is why I don't have to write Christian music… thanks for listening Mr. Mailman*). Still, no one would argue with me. No one would tell me for sure, one way or the other, whether I could, or couldn't, continue writing secular songs and remain with my band. It probably didn't matter much to most of them, but it mattered to me… a lot. They would listen patiently, see my points and tell me things like, "Ok, well, maybe you should pray about it," or ask, "What do you think God is trying to tell you?" I hated that. Those responses seemed to me to be either a way to brush me off, or to manipulate me, as if praying about it could result in only one answer, but, truthfully, I was looking for an argument from people, not counsel. I wanted to fight, but who was I fighting? In reality, I was fighting with God.

The disturbing thing was that, during this whole struggle, I couldn't write a song to save my life. I tried, but couldn't pen anything of worth. This was a big deal because, in my musical life, I took great pride in writing songs. It's what I did; it's who I was. So, when I couldn't write a song, it frustrated me beyond measure. It felt like God was working behind the scenes, draining my inspiration pool, that place inside me where I'd always gone at will to draw out new songs. My dry spell lasted months, and I was thirsty and irritated.

I lived across the street from a golf course. I used to go out at night with my dog and acoustic guitar to write, (the dog had the greatest ideas) but my writing sessions there had become more like venting sessions. I would try to write, and, when nothing would come, I'd pour out my frustrations with God to God. Looking back, it seems so foolish. I was angry with God for "taking away my ability to write." There I was, in the middle of a darkened fairway, my black lab cocking her puzzled head at me, while, with a guitar in one fist, I shook the other at heaven. I'd yell, "Why can't I write anymore?" or, "You want me to write songs for you, don't you?" It was rather arrogant and more than a little crazy. I definitely do *not* advise this practice, especially out in a golf course where lightening can easily strike.

When I came to Christ, I knew I'd be making some sacrifices, but I just didn't know how great some sacrifices would be. I was so closely wrapped into my music that I felt like I was dying, and God was the one killing me… killing, not only my dreams, but my very identity.

I came to a point of realization. I would either receive his plan—his uncomfortable, annoying, seemingly music-less plan—or return to my own selfish way of life. Even though I didn't like how it felt, or the package it came in, I didn't want to miss my opportunity to be in God's will. This was the day of his visitation in my life; therefore, if I trusted that God was good, and that he knew best, then I would have to accept any package that the Lord, in his infinite wisdom, grace and mercy, chose to deliver.

LIFE APPLICATIONS:

1. What are some preconceived notions you have, or had of God? How have these shaped your life choices?

_____

_____

_____

_____

_____

_____

_____

_____

_____

_____

2. Describe a time in your life where there was a tension between what you wanted for your life and what God wanted for your life. What was the outcome?

_____

_____

_____

_____

_____

_____

_____

_____

_____

_____

Which do you believe?

☐—God has a plan in the world; my purpose in life is to be part of it.

☐—I have a plan in life and God will help me fulfill it.

Explain.

_____

_____

_____

_____

_____

_____

_____

_____

_____

_____

4

 ## DEN OF THEIVES

Matthew 21:12-16

Then, Jesus went into the temple of God and drove out all those who bought and sold in it, and overturned the tables of the moneychangers and the seats of those who sold doves. And he said to them, "It is written, 'My house shall be called a house of prayer,' but you have made it a 'den of thieves.'"

Then, the blind and the lame came to him in the temple, and he healed them. But when the chief priests and scribes saw the wonderful things that he did, and the children crying out in the temple and saying, "Hosanna to the son of David!" They were indignant and said to him, "Do you hear what these are saying?"

And Jesus said to them, "Yes. Have you never read: 'Out of the mouth of babes and nursing infants, You have perfected praise?'"

A CLEAN HOUSE

The temple was built as a central place for worship, teaching, repentance and prayer, a holy place where God reveals his presence, and the path of faith, grace and mercy that leads the sinner to him. To call it a holy place means that it is not to be used for any purpose other than the service of God, as he set his spirit there. After visiting the Jerusalem temple three times a year for decades, Jesus finally decides to publically address its growing religious debauchery. Quoting Isaiah 56:7, Jesus begins to clean house, kicking over tables and lashing the temple's defilers. He says, "It is written, 'My house shall be called a house of prayer,' but you have made it a 'den of thieves.'" The image is poignant for them. This area of Israel is filled with caves, which served the secret purposes of revolutionaries and thieves alike, huddling in their dens and going out to mischief. Under the authority of the present priestly rulers, the temple had become a racket designed to use the pressure of religious power to fleece the worshipers who came from afar to honor God. Jesus had had enough. He was taking it back for God, getting out what had no place there, and calling for the restoration of its divinely decreed holy functions.

After church, on the day I gave my life to Christ, my friends, David and Shelby, drove us back to my house. Our band, as I mentioned earlier, had played the night before, and so some of our friends, those who would come out to see us regularly, had partied and crashed at my house. They were all still asleep when we got back. Dave and I proceeded to wake everyone up and get them out of the house.

The place stank of stale booze and cigarettes. Empty beer bottles and ashtrays filled with crumpled cigarette butts were everywhere. We filled two large trash bags to bursting with the stuff and took to cleaning the whole house. We mopped the floors, washed the tables, reset the furniture, and vacuumed the rugs, and, all the while, I remember thinking how perfectly symbolic it was; if my day had been a movie, you could hardly have scripted a better closing scene. God was cleaning up my life.

THE TEMPLE

We, individually and corporately, are called *the temple* of God in the New Testament. Paul writes, "Do you not know that your body is the temple of the Holy Spirit who is in you, whom you have from God, and you are not your own?" (1 Corinthians 6:10; also 3:16-17) and "What agreement does a temple of God have with idols? For you are the temple of the living God, as God has said, 'I will dwell in them and walk among *them*; and I will be their God, and they shall be my people.'" (2 Corinthians 6:16) This idea stands initially behind the creation story itself, where man, as the image of God, is filled with his Spirit, a vessel into which he puts his breath.

God wants to make you and I his temple, but there are things that just don't belong in us, so he wants to clean the place. When I came to Christ, there were many sinful and profane practices that had to go. Some went right away, but others took some time, and he is still at it with me. He still cleans out what shouldn't be there, so I can be devoted to his purposes. The technical term for this process is called *sanctification.*

Sanctification is a fancy word that means *separated for his use.* Think of it this way: If I have a golden bowl that I use to burn incense to the Lord, I can't take that bowl and go home and eat my Fruity Pebbles in it. It is separated for the use of burning incense. In the same way, Christ wants us to be cleansed and separated for his use, and this means that we become undefiled in the devotion of our lives.

THE RESPONSES

Not everybody responds to Jesus' work in the same way. Here, in our text, we see three different groups with three different responses to the work of Jesus: the blind and the lame, the children, and the scribes and chief priests.

The blind and lame respond to the work of Jesus by simply coming to him. They understand their condition, and they know who Jesus is; so, they come to him in faith, receiving healing.

The children respond with praise.

The scribes and the chief priests, however, are "indignant" with Christ. You may find it hard to believe that religious folks would get that upset over people being healed and children lifting their voices in praise, but that is their response of choice. They are proud of their positions of authority and the influence that they have over the people; thus, they find only displeasure and irritation with the word and work of the Lord.

I can't help but see the relevance of these responses to the cleansing work of Christ. We all respond in different ways to Jesus at different times. Sometimes, we may be like the lame and blind, coming to him in need, believing and desperate for the Lord's work in our lives. Sometimes, we may respond in childlike faith and wonder, giving praise to God for his surprising work. Sometimes, however, we scoff and grow indignant at his attempts to set us right. This passage reminds us to take inventory of the things that we may be allowing into our spiritual temple. We are reminded to check our responses, because if there are things in our spiritual temple that don't belong, it's always best to allow him in to do some house cleaning.

LIFE APPLICATIONS:

1. Name some things in the temple of your life that you imagine need to be cleansed?

_____

_____

_____

_____

_____

_____

_____

_____

_____

_____

2. Have you ever experienced a time in your life when you felt like Christ was cleansing you? If so, describe the experience.

_____

_____

_____

_____

_____

_____

_____

_____

_____

_____

3. Who best describes your response to past attempts by Christ to cleanse things from your life? The desperate and grateful blind and lame? The praising children? The indignant and resistant chief priests and Pharisees? Explain.

_____

_____

_____

_____

_____

_____

_____

_____

_____

_____

5

WHO IS THIS MAN?

Luke 19:45-48

Then He went into the temple and began to drive out those who bought and sold in it, saying to them, "It is written, 'My house is a house of prayer,'" but you have made it a den of thieves. He was teaching daily in the temple. But the chief priests, the scribes, and the leaders of the people sought to destroy him, and were unable to do anything; because all the people were very attentive to hear him.

John 11:47-48; 53

Then, the chief priests and the Pharisees gathered a council and said, "What shall we do? For this man works many signs. If we let him alone like this, everyone will believe in him, and the Romans will come and take away both our place and nation."

Then, from that day on, they plotted to put him to death.

A THREAT

The religious leaders of the people sought to destroy Jesus by attempting to alter his identity. They came up with all kinds of ideas. They could make Jesus out to be a conjurer, a blasphemer, a liar, a fraud, etc. Even though they witnessed Jesus' miracles, heard his teachings and observed the influence he had over the people, these leaders didn't see him as the Christ, (i.e. anticipated kingly SAVIOR... Messiah) instead they saw him as a threat. They cared little for who he actually was, concerned more with who they could make him out to be. They fumble over themselves, grasping for some suitable false identity they could use to frame Jesus.

The leaders of Israel had serious material stakes in the corrupt goings-on of the temple. They also had great influence and all the twisted emotional rewards that such power gives to those who know how to abuse it. Doves and other animals were used in part of the temple worship, but they were hard to transport, so one's sacrificial animals could be sold and replaced with animals purchased at the temple. The temple leaders, of course, had a higher mark-up on their products than Disney®, netting large profits for all involved. They also instituted a temple tax that had to be paid with Jewish money. Those coming from afar, who could only get their hands on Roman coin, had to exchange their money at the temple, garnering the money changers and the temple leaders even more profits through egregious fees.

The Jewish people were a volatile bunch, wound tight with messianic fervor, waiting anxiously for deliverance from their Roman oppressors. The Jewish rulers, like the Sadducees and Pharisees, however, had a rather ambiguous relationship with the Romans. They had obtained positions of power and wealth under the Romans' odious rule. So, when Christ cleared the temple, he threatened the status quo; he risked riots that the Romans would be forced to quell, perhaps, costing these leaders their positions. Messiah may have been a vague hope for freedom from oppression to some of them, but was a threat of loss of position, wealth and comfort to others. The work of God will always provoke hatred, and all that comes with it, from those whose emotional, mental, and material designs stand at cross purposes to God's character, will and plan.

"I HATED YOU"

There were a lot of voices in my life when I came to Christ. My friends and my band were much like a family. So, *my* life changes impacted their lives in material and immaterial ways. I can remember those early conversations with my bandmates and close friends; they started out with sarcastic questions like, "So, what? Are you, like, a 'born again' now, or something?" They went downhill from there. They figured that I had "imagined the whole thing," or that I'd "been brainwashed." I was talking with a friend about the Lord one night. I explained that it was as if I had found a treasure of gold and was trying to get him to come and see for himself. He merely quipped, "Yeah! Sure! Gold... more like fool's gold." My friends began to make it a personal mission to tempt me, to get me to slip up in some way, to test the strength of my resolve. One close friend distanced himself from me, confessing later, "I hated you when you became a born-again Christian." I was shocked because I cared a lot more about him since my encounter with Christ. I was, for the first time, overtly seeking to love and care for him. Then, I realized that he really didn't hate me. How could he? I didn't do anything directly to him. Perhaps, it was God whom he hated. Perhaps, I just represented his enemy.

ENMITY

The apostles spoke often about man's hostility toward God. James wrote, "Do you not know that the friendship of the world is enmity with God? Therefore, whoever desires to be a friend of the world is the enemy of God." (James 4:4) Paul concurs, saying, "...because the carnal mind is enmity against God, for it is not subject to the Law of God, neither indeed can it be." (Romans 8:7) Peter regarded hatred from the lost toward the Christian a natural condition, saying, "Beloved, do not be astonished at the fiery trial which is to try you, as though a strange thing happened to you... If you are reviled for the name of Christ, you are blessed, because the Spirit of God and of glory rests on you. (1 Peter 4:12-14) Jesus said it himself, first, "If the world hates you, you know that it hated me before it hated you. If you were of the world, the world would love its own. But because you are not of the world, but I have chosen you out of the world, therefore the world hates you. Remember the word that I said to you, the servant is not greater than his master. If they have persecuted me, they will also persecute you. If they have kept my saying, they will also keep yours. But all these things they will do to you for my name's sake, because they do not know him who sent me." (John 15:18-21)

When Jesus sought to restore the temple to God's purposes, the religious leaders' profit and power were threatened. When I sought to restore the temple of my life to God's purpose, the profit and hopes of my friends were threatened. My new way of life was a hazard to their old way of life. My bandmates had a stake in the future of our group and the music we had written. We'd put our lives into the vision and the goals of the band. Their everything was on the line.

In the past, their adverse reactions to, and their belittlement of, my changed life would have provoked me to lash out through wounded pride. Knowing the cause of their hostility helped me respond with loving and understanding concern. I received grace when I was at enmity with God; shouldn't they, even if I get caught in the crossfire? The light bulb had gone on—those who have received God's grace must also become extensions of his grace.

LIFE APPLICATIONS:

1. Has there been a time when you responded angrily, or negatively when someone's life changed for the better? How did they respond? Was their response helpful to you? How so?

_____

_____

_____

_____

_____

_____

_____

_____

_____

_____

2. Has there been a time when others responded angrily, or negatively when you've made a positive spiritual change in your life? Give details. How did you respond?

_____

_____

_____

_____

_____

_____

_____

_____

_____

_____

3. In what way might a gracious response to negative, or, even, hostile reactions to a spiritually changed life help others in their own spiritual journey? Explain.

_____

_____

_____

_____

_____

_____

_____

_____

_____

_____

4. How does the understanding of the hostility towards God that Christ and the apostles spoke about give you perspective on persecution? What might a helpful response to persecution look like?

_____

_____

_____

_____

_____

_____

_____

_____

_____

_____

6

TELL US TEACHER

Matthew 21:23-27

Now when Jesus came into the temple, the chief priests and the elders of the people confronted him as he was teaching, and said, "By what authority are you doing these things? And who gave you this authority?"

But Jesus answered and said to them, "I also will ask you one thing, which if you tell me, I likewise will tell you by what authority I do these things: The baptism of John— where was it from? From heaven or from men?"

And they reasoned among themselves, saying, "If we say, 'From heaven,' he will say to us, 'Why then did you not believe him?' But if we say, 'From men,' we fear the multitude, for all count John as a prophet."

So they answered Jesus and said, "We do not know."

And he said to them, "Neither will I tell you by what authority I do these things."

CANNOT OR WILL NOT?

Jesus is making quite a fuss and interfering in the affairs of the temple, and these leaders demand to know by what authority he claims the right to challenge the temple practices. Jesus is not a priest; he isn't a Pharisee, nor a scribe, nor a Sadducee. In fact, he has no civil or ecclesiastical authority of any kind. Large numbers of the people are listening to him because he presents himself as a prophet and works miracles, which make this a potentially volatile and dangerous situation for the temple leaders. They themselves, of course, care nothing for such claims, and are, apparently, little impressed with wonders. They care more about other things, like power and the material benefits of power. *Who is he to act like he rules the place?* So they ask him, "By what authority are you doing these things? And who gave you this authority?"

They want Jesus to make some open claim before witnesses that they can use against him, to destroy him, caring little for his answers beyond that. These are not honest questions, and Jesus, never one to play their games by their rules, turns the tables on them. As if to say, "Authority? Yeah… let's talk about *authority*."

He will force *them* to make a claim that will expose their corruption. What do you make of John the Baptist's authority? Divine? Human? Did John come preaching and baptizing based solely on his own manipulative personal power over people, working a personality cult? Did John come as the representative of God, to whom belongs all power and all authority? Given the volatility of the people and the popularity of John the Baptist, they don't dare denounce John, but, if they say John's authority came from God, they would need to explain their resistance to John's message, and, hence, to the message and work of Jesus, whom they are presently seeking to destroy.

This has been the question of the ages; with Christ as the fulcrum of human history, will you deny Jesus' authority, or will you recognize and accept his authority as incarnate deity? It is an issue of Lordship. If he is not who he says he is, has not come from where he says he's come, then denounce him utterly; he is either a complete madman or the greatest cheat in the millennia of man. If he is who he says he is, has come from where he says he's come, then there is no middle ground, no room for lukewarm response, no place for half-hearted obedience. As the adage goes, "Jesus is either Lord of all, or he's not Lord at all."

QUESTIONING AUTHORITY

I was confronted with this authority and lordship issue early on in my Christian walk. The problem I faced was that I knew he wanted more of me—all of me, actually. I knew he wanted to utilize my musical talents for him, but I fought and fought. This may seem a small thing, but my music, at the time, was my life; my whole identity was wrapped up in it; my whole sense of forward direction was built on it—*my* music, *my* plans, *my* life. As noted, I tried to justify *my* plan, seeking a word of peace from others to justify my disobedience, but I only wore people out with my bleating.

Looking back on my past struggle, it was as if the Lord had, since my conversion experience, been standing outside my condemned, dilapidated house with a wrecking crew and wrecking ball, with a megaphone saying, "Please come out of the house." I heard him for sure, but I didn't want to leave the comfort of my old house. *Okay*, I thought, *my house is a little drafty; the roof leaks, and, alright, the foundation's cracked; the paint's peeling, and the stairs are broken; yeah, yeah, there are holes in the walls and the floor boards are rotted; birds are nesting in the rafters; yes, I suppose it is infested with termites, and, maybe smells kind of bad, but this is my house! I have great plans for it. I have so many memories here.*

Recognizing his authority in truth, and submitting to him, meant that he'd claim the deed, pull the permit to wreck and rebuild my house. He'd call the shots, draw up the blueprints, supply the laborers and materials, and oversee the job until complete. I just didn't have enough faith to trust his work, yet. I didn't know what my life would look like if I submitted completely to his authority. I feared the worst, so I stayed in the house. He could have turned to his wrecking crew and said, "Ok boys, pack it up, he's not coming out. Let's go home." He could have left me there, watching out of my drafty windows as he drove off, wrecking ball in tow, leaving me to rot in my worthless house.

There is a Scripture that says, "And the Lord said, 'My Spirit shall not always strive with man, in his erring.'" (Genesis 6:3) In truth, he did not strive always with these religious rulers, who refused to acknowledge that God's authority sustained John's work, and who plotted murder through their jealous hatred of Jesus, God's Messiah, man's SAVIOR.

Let me encourage you, though. If the Lord is dealing with you, do yourself a favor and submit to his *authority*. Allow him to be your Lord. Grant him access to every area of your life. Let *him* pull the permit; then, get out of the house. Leave it behind and watch him bring it down and build something new.

LIFE APPLICATIONS:

1. By what authority do you believe Jesus acted? Was he a liar, a lunatic, or Lord of all, as he claimed? On what do you base your answer?

_____

_____

_____

_____

_____

_____

_____

_____

_____

_____

_____

2. Who do you feel has full authority in your life right now—you or God? Is there anything that you are consciously holding back from God? Explain.

_____

_____

_____

_____

_____

_____

_____

_____

_____

3. What do you imagine your life would look like if you submitted completely to Jesus Christ's authority?

_____

_____

_____

_____

_____

_____

_____

_____

_____

_____

7

PARABLE OF THE TENANTS

Luke 20:9-12

Then, he began to tell the people this parable: "A certain man planted a vineyard, leased it to vinedressers, and went into a far country for a long time. Now at vintage-time, he sent a servant to the vinedressers, that they might give him some of the fruit of the vineyard. But the vinedressers beat him and sent him away empty-handed. Again, he sent another servant; and they beat him also, treated him shamefully, and sent him away empty-handed. And, again, he sent a third; and they wounded him also and cast him out.

Then, last of all, he sent his son to them, saying, 'They will respect my son.' But when the vinedressers saw the son, they said among themselves, 'This is the heir. Come, let us kill him and seize his inheritance.' So they took him and cast him out of the vineyard and killed him.

Therefore, when the owner of the vineyard comes, what will he do to those vinedressers?"

They said to him, "He will destroy those wicked men miserably, and lease his vineyard to other vinedressers who will render to him the fruits in their seasons."

PARABLES

Jesus was the greatest teacher. He regularly used analogical stories, or parables to illustrate a spiritual lesson. Christ had a statement that he often would attach to his parables, "If anyone has ears to hear, let him hear." I always liked that expression. It was his way of saying, "Those of you who are really listening and getting what I am saying, be sure you take it to heart." I used a variation of Christ's saying as the chorus of this song. "So to you who have ears to hear, won't you hear?" because it is so easy to listen to a song, or a parable like this one without understanding its meaning.

A quick look at Jesus' audience shows us the type of characters represented in his parable. "And on one of those days, as he taught the people in the temple and proclaimed the gospel, it happened that the chief priests and the scribes along with the elders came up." (Luke 20:1) "And he began to speak to the people this parable: A certain man planted a vineyard... " (Luke 20:9) In the setting of the Bible, this was a sensible story. Given the ancient prophets' frequent description of Israel in arboreal pictures, a tale of a vineyard was easily imagined.

The Lord (vineyard owner) established Israel (vineyard) and left its mission in the hands of Abraham's descendants (vinedressers), much of whose course is being charted by present Jewish religious leaders (vinedressers). The Lord wants this mission fulfilled (the fruit of the vineyard) and sends his prophets (servants) to claim it. Throughout the history of Israel, they have rejected and murdered his prophets (servants). God has now sent Jesus (son) to demand obedience to his covenant, which they have cast off (refused to give fruit). They will kill Jesus (son) who, through his death, will establish a new covenant (owner takes away their place, gives it to others).

Beyond the prophetic implications of this parable for Jesus' historic audience, we also see, here, a grand picture of divine stewardship in general. A steward is one who takes charge of something on behalf of its owner, fulfilling the owner's purposes with it. God, creator, is owner of all, and, as such, has a proper expectation that each of his creatures uses what he has given them, as he has purposed. Your days, your hands, your eyes, and, yes, those other parts, too, all belong to him. He has set down a path for you in his holy word. He has provided his Holy Spirit as enabler and guide. He expects you to govern your days, your hands, your eyes, and, yes, those other parts, too, according to his purposes. This is the fruit of it.

DO YOU WANT TO GO TO HEAVEN?

When I was twenty years old, my stepfather died from cancer. During his last days, a woman came to our house to help my mom take care of him. She was a kind, but intense, type of Christian, a great blessing to us during this difficult time. We talked a lot, and she would often start up spiritual conversations with me. At the time, I had little concern for the things of God, but was more than a little concerned about my stepfather and my mother. She saw my anxiety and would constantly invite me to her church.

She knew I was heavily into music, so, she would say, "You've got to come to my church and hear 'our band'; they're awesome!" She was thoughtful, and wise to appeal to my musical interests, but the very idea of a church band was comically ironic to me. I was raised Catholic, and old New England Catholic churches were the only mental picture I had of *church*. Images of a rock band cranking it out in an old stone sanctuary seemed ridiculous, and unappealing, to say the least. But I always told her I would go, without any real intention of doing so. I didn't see any need to go to church. She, obviously, cared enough to regularly invite me, and I didn't want to hurt her feelings.

One day, we were in my kitchen, and she asked me a straight up question—"Jonathan, do you want to go to heaven?"

What do you say to that? "Sure," I replied.

"Then, go upstairs in your room and get that big Bible of yours (I've had it since my first communion; it was thicker than a New York Phone Directory) and bring it down here." So, reluctantly, I did as she asked. She sat me down at the kitchen table and opened the big Bible. She sifted through a few crackling pages, read a scripture I can't remember, and had me recite a prayer after her. Then, she looked up at me and yelled, "Praise God, you're going to heaven!" She was obviously excited, but I had no idea what had just happened. I put the Bible back on my shelf and thought, *Well, that's done. I Guess*

I'm going to heaven now. And that was it. Like I'd just checked, "Be Sure to Go To Heaven," off my bucket list. Then, nothing happened. My life continued as it had. God sent her to me, but in reality, polite as I tried to be, I rejected her and her message. I had no interest in giving God the fruit of his own vineyard. I continued to lay claim to it as my own.

Interestingly enough, a short time before I actually came to Christ, I was talking with Brian, the drummer of my band, about writing music for God. I told him that if we didn't use our talents for God, that he could take it all away. It dawned on us that, if God was calling us, and we wouldn't listen, he had every right to seize any gift that he had given to us. This was my first realization of stewardship—God gives for the purpose of his harvest.

GOD'S SERVANTS

That day, when Dave and Shelby arrived in my basement and spoke to us about the gospel of Christ, I told them that I believed in God. When Shelby asked me directly, "Where is the *fruit* of that?" I had to ask myself, *Of all the things my life produced, what part of it validated my claim to believe in God?* I gave him nothing of what I produced, and produced nothing of what he'd purposed me to produce.

Thankfully, God is a patient loving Father, who may send many of his servants to us, even though we keep abusing them. The final test will be what we do with his son, Jesus.

After I gave my life to Christ, I wanted to find that eager servant of God who had been such a faithful witness for Jesus in my dark hours. I remembered the church she attended, because she told me where it was a million times. When I walked in, far from an old craggy stone cathedral, I found a large modern church building seating over a thousand people; I thought, *How on earth am I going to find her?* When the pastor had the congregation sit and bow their heads to pray, however, I could see her sitting up near the front. Exactly, where I might have suspected she'd be if I'd thought about it. I snuck up quietly, slipped into the vacant seat behind her and gently tapped her on the shoulder. She turned around and shouted at the top of her lungs, "Oh, my God!" As everyone turned to look, she threw her arms around me, and I laughed.

LIFE APPLICATIONS:

1. Has God sent his servants into your life? If so, what has been your response to them? In what way is God sending you as his servant into his harvest field?

_____

_____

_____

_____

_____

_____

_____

_____

_____

_____

2. What kind of fruit have you been growing in the garden of your life? For whom have you been growing it?

_____

_____

_____

_____

_____

_____

_____

_____

_____

_____

3. How have you been rejecting the Son and his message from your life, in thought and in deed?

_____

_____

_____

_____

_____

_____

_____

_____

_____

_____

_____

4. What are some things you could change, with the Lord's help, to be more spiritually productive?

_____

_____

_____

_____

_____

_____

_____

_____

_____

_____

_____

8

THE PRODIGAL SON

Luke 15:11-32

"A certain man had two sons. And the younger of them said to his father, 'Father, give me the portion of goods that falls to me.' So he divided to him his livelihood. And not many days after, the younger son gathered all together, journeyed to a far country, and there wasted his possessions with prodigal living. But when he had spent all, there arose a severe famine in that land, and he began to be in want. Then, he went and joined himself to a citizen of that country, and he sent him into his fields to feed swine. And he would gladly have filled his stomach with the pods that the swine ate, and no one gave him anything.

But when he came to himself, he said, 'How many of my father's hired servants have bread enough and to spare, and I perish with hunger! I will arise and go to my father, and will say to him, 'Father, I have sinned against heaven and before you, and I am no longer worthy to be called your son. Make me like one of your hired servants.'

And he arose and came to his father. But when he was still a great way off, his father saw him and had compassion, and ran and fell on his neck and kissed him. And the son said to him, 'Father, I have sinned against heaven and in your sight, and am no longer worthy to be called your son.'

But the father said to his servants, 'Bring out the best robe and put it on him, and put a ring on his hand and sandals on his feet. And bring the fatted calf here and kill it, and let us eat and be merry; for this my son was dead and is alive again; he was lost and is found.' And they began to be merry.'

Now his older son was in the field. And as he came and drew near to the house, he heard music and dancing. So he called one of the servants and asked what these things meant. And he said to him, 'Your brother has come, and because he has received him safe and sound, your father has killed the fatted calf.'

But he was angry and would not go in. Therefore, his father came out and pleaded with him. So he answered and said to *his* father, 'Lo, these many years I have been serving you; I never transgressed your commandment at any time; and yet you never gave me a young goat, that I might make merry with my friends. But as soon as this son of yours came, who has devoured your livelihood with harlots, you killed the fatted calf for him.'

And he said to him, 'Son, you are always with me, and all that I have is yours. It was right that we should make merry and be glad, for your brother was dead and is alive again, and was lost and is found.'"

PRODIGAL LIVING

I can't remember a time that I didn't want to play the guitar. At the age of thirteen, my endless pestering finally convinced my dad to get me a black electric Fender Stratocaster, a small amp and guitar lessons. I poured myself into practice, riding my bike for miles, guitar on my back, to my lessons. Before long, I started hanging around with some older guys in real bands. They listened to and played some pretty heavy music, which I soon learned to play. I began to live and breathe heavy metal.

This introduced me to some shady places and even shadier older musicians. I idolized these guys; they were 'cool.' They swore, smoked, had sex and drank, and I wanted to live my life this way too, to get away from the restraints of my parents and find my identity in my music.

I was about fourteen years old when my father caught me smoking and drinking. My parents had been divorced since I was three, and I lived with my dad in Providence. A friend and I got a neighbor to buy us a six-pack of beer, and we split it behind a church (of all places), while we smoked.

I knew when I came home that I'd need to hide the smell. We lived on the top floor of a three-story tenement, so I stashed mouth wash and a change of clothes in the vacant second floor apartment beneath us, and crept into it before going upstairs. As I slunk out, my father met me on the landing.

He had a suspicious look in his eyes, as if peering into my soul. He asked why I was creeping into the house; he was on to me. I concocted a stupid story, but my dad just said, "Let me smell your breath." I guess the mouth wash didn't help… I was busted. He brought me down the street to my friend's house, hollered at both of us, then grounded me.

I was humiliated and super angry. I wanted to do what I wanted to do, whenever and however I wanted to do it. In the following days and weeks, I grew determined to escape my father's house. One day, without telling my father, I ran away… and moved in with my mom. What a rebel! I imagined I could get away with more at her house, and so I spent the next ten years living as a prodigal son.

THE PARABLE

Prodigal means to be reckless or wasteful. It begins with a mentality that throws off restraint. Christ is talking to a mixed crowd of prodigal sons and religious elitists, doers and non-doers, law-keepers and law-breakers, the Pharisees and the sinners. Jesus has been hanging out with the "sinners and tax-collectors," and is catching flack for welcoming these prodigals home. So, Jesus tells this parable to describe the heart of the Father towards both of his wayward children.

THE WAYWARD SON

The younger son seems to have it good in his father's house. So, why leave? Like me, this son imagines there is something to be gained by a life without restraint. I get it. If you breathe oxygen and live on planet earth, I'm sure you get it. It's "the-grass-is-greener" syndrome, the "if-only" imaginings of the dissatisfied. This son believes that an unrestrained, reckless life of sin will fulfill his dreams.

Sin, however, is a hook in the jaw. It aims to drag us into darkness, into mental, physical and spiritual dregs, but that's not sin's first impression. Sin presents itself shiny and bright on the first date, lovely and perfect. It's the beautiful fruit of Eve's desire. That's the lure. I felt it. The Prodigal feels it. I'm sure you've felt it—the pull to leave the Father's house to indulge fantasies without care for the consequences.

Giving in to temptation is like trying to put out a fire with gasoline. Just so, Jesus uses the illustration of a famine to depict sin's degrading force. Sin burns away our lives, depleting our resources and emotions, and corrupting our mentalities, until we're sitting in a sty, like the prodigal, longing even for what the pigs are eating.

THE LOVE OF THE FATHER

At this point of the story, the *do-gooders* in Jesus' audience are probably happy that this disobedient son is getting what he deserves. Then, Jesus gives the turn, saying that the prodigal "*came to himself*"— the transformation of a heart summed up in one powerful phrase… but what caused his heart to turn? It was the remembrance of the goodness of his father's house. So, he gets up, tattered, shameful, dirty, and pungent as a pig and walks home.

Hoping for no more than the mercy of working as his father's servant, he rehearses a speech, making confession without the hope of forgiveness. He is shocked, however, when his father runs to him, embraces him and kisses him. The son tries to give his speech, but it's ignored as his father orders his servants to fetch a robe, a ring and shoes… to prepare a feast.

THE OTHER WAYWARD SON

The older brother, the *do-gooder*, is out in the field doing what good responsible older brothers do—he is working. Then, he hears dancing and smells a barbecue… is shocked to learn that it is for his no-good younger brother. He is angry and refuses to come into the house to join the party. So, the father comes out to him, as well.

The older brother has his own speech, highlighting his good deeds, his good behavior. It's as if the older son is saying, "Hey, Dad, guess what? While this son of yours was out being the prodigal, living it up with prostitutes, guess what I've been doing? I've been WORKING! I've been *doing,* and you throw *him* a feast?! You should be punishing him! Why are you treating him like this? Why are you treating me like this?"

That's the question isn't it? Why love and forgiveness? …and if that, why painful obedience?

This righteous brother, however, whatever he may imagine, has something significant in common with his prodigal brother. They both believe their father's love is earned by good behavior and performance. One son is far away from the father's house, while the other is close, but both have the same misconception of entitlement and self-justification, both miss the heart of their father, imagining that his love is conditional.

The older son's speech is virtually ignored, as well. Instead, the father reveals his heart. "Son, you are always with me, and all that I have is yours. It was right that we should make merry and be glad, for your brother was dead and is alive again, and was lost and is found." (Luke 15:31-32) This is the answer to the question of forgiveness and obedience—he loves them and wants them to be *with* him.

Like these sons, we can be far from home and misunderstand the heart of God, or we can be close to home and miss it just as easily. Our attitudes about our actions can be obstacles that keep us from being with him in meaningful relationship. Our attitudes about our bad behavior can hold us back from repenting and turning to him, afraid that we cannot earn back his love. Our attitudes about our good behavior can also be an obstacle, keeping us from seeing our need, from recognizing the true horror of our sin, certain that we, unlike those around us, have earned the father's love. The father's desire is that we share his heart for others. The prodigal was right in this way; none of us are worthy of the Father's forgiveness. Thankfully, being with him is not about our worth, it's about his love, mercy and grace… always.

LIFE APPLICATIONS:

1. Think of a time where you fled from God like the prodigal son. Think of a time when you were tempted to anger like the brother. Think of a time when you had the chance to extend the mercy of the father. To which of the characters in this parable to you best relate? Why?

_____

_____

_____

_____

_____

_____

_____

_____

_____

_____

2. Has there ever been a moment in your life when you felt like you "came to yourself"? Explain.

_____

_____

_____

_____

_____

_____

_____

_____

_____

_____

3. How has your attitude about your actions and/or the actions of others affected your relationship with God? Have they caused distance or closeness with God?

_____

_____

_____

_____

_____

_____

_____

_____

_____

_____

4. Think of something important that you have lost and then found, or loved so dearly, that it gives you some sense of insight into the heart of the father for his lost sons and daughters. How does this affect your attitude towards God and others?

_____

_____

_____

_____

_____

_____

_____

_____

_____

_____

9

THEY CALL HIM TEACHER

John 11:47-48; 53

Then, the chief priests and the Pharisees gathered a council and said, "What shall we do? For this man works many signs. If we let him alone like this, everyone will believe in him, and the Romans will come and take away both our place and nation.

Then, from that day on, they plotted to put him to death.

Matthew 21:45-46

Now when the chief priests and Pharisees heard his parables, they perceived that he was speaking of them. But when they sought to lay hands on him, they feared the multitudes, because they took him for a prophet.

BEHIND CLOSED DOORS

Let's talk about change. Let's talk about the things that we will hold on to, the things that we will do in order to keep from having to change. If we can define culture simply as "the way things are done around here," then how do we respond typically when something from the outside comes in to challenge our status quo, provoking change?

In a closed door session, (a session that has a certain affinity with many a secret meeting of today, held on a daily basis in our own neighborhoods, businesses, churches, in parking lots, phone calls, on

Facebook, etc.) we find different sorts of religious leaders in Israel offended and gathered together to figure a way to ensnare Jesus without provoking the masses. Jesus comes preaching counter-cultural kingdom principles that threaten "the ways things are done around here," provoking change. Rather than dealing with Jesus honestly, or redemptively, these leaders are blinded by their fear, jealousy and hatred, creating emotional tunnel vision with only one end in sight. They become deceitful, niggling, argumentative, and conniving schemers, supplanting the truth to preserve "the way the things are done around here."

This song from SAVIOR gives a musical view of what it may have been like behind those closed-door sessions. We can imagine the tone of the conversation—*Hey! Why don't we set a trap for him in front of the people*—*"by his own words, and by his own lies, we'll catch him and they'll see for sure behind the disguise."* (Perhaps, without the rhyme scheme.) If they could trip him up, Jesus might either look stupid, or the crowds could be provoked to rage, or his answers might provide them the legal justification to accuse him. Either way, they had to stop him, discredit him, because he was a direct threat to their culture. So, they have a *great idea*; they send in The A-Team, the heavy hitters, religious special forces sent to ambush Jesus with trick questions. From *Matthew 22:15-46,* we have a picture of this ambush.

JESUS-1—A-TEAM-0

First come The Herodians, political loyalists to king Herod. They want to know if it is right for Jews to pay taxes to Caesar—a rather unpopular position. Say, "YES" to taxes, and the people will turn against him as a Roman sympathizer. Say, "NO" to taxes, and he can be accused before the Romans as an insurrectionist.

Jesus, however, points away from earthly concerns and toward spiritual ones. If Caesar's stamped image makes the denarius his in the first place, then what bears God's image that those seeking to trap him should give to God? Answer: Themselves.

JESUS-2—A-TEAM-0

Next up are the Sadducees, the high priestly families who govern the temple. Seeking to make the idea of resurrection (a theological point of contention between themselves and the Pharisees) look absurd, the Sadducees work up a silly picture of it based on false assumptions from the Law of Moses regarding marriage and the afterlife. This approach is common even today—The Straw Man Argument. Jesus, refusing to play their game, goes to the root of their problem. They don't know the Scriptures, and they don't know the power of God. Those who come asking mocking questions of God and his Word rarely come to a true knowledge of either.

JESUS-3—A-TEAM-0

When the Pharisees hear that he has silenced the Sadducees, they send in the lawyers. Issues of "light" versus "heavy" commands were a common point of debate among the legal experts; so, they ask which is the greatest command in Scripture—a question designed to expose Jesus' lack of academic finesse and to offend the people who often divide from others over seemingly insignificant points in the Law.

Jesus, true to form, simplifies their seemingly complex issue. He chooses two commands that, far from being in tension with others, stand as the theological and practical wellspring of them all:

"Hear, O Israel: The LORD our God, the LORD is one. You shall love the LORD your God with all your heart and with all your soul and with all your might." (Deuteronomy 6:4-5) and "You shall not take vengeance or bear a grudge against the sons of your own people, but you shall love your neighbor as yourself: I am the LORD." (Leviticus 19:18)

GAME, SET, MATCH

While the Pharisees are gathered together, (probably trying to devise their next attack) Jesus confronts and confounds them, exposing their own ignorance, with a question regarding Messiah and his relationship to his father, David, being both his descendent and

56

his master.

Jesus turns in Matthew 23 to speak to the masses about these men. As earthly rulers, their positions should be honored, their commands obeyed, but do not follow their examples. They seek praise of men not God and are unfit for their positions as hypocritical oppressors. These leaders should come to submit, to learn and to humble themselves before the one to whom even David bent his knee. Instead, because of their rage and bias, they come to Christ to trap, to confound and to humiliate and, consequently, get nowhere. Questions with faith lead to learning. Questions with a mocking, stubborn, incredulous and proud heart lead to nothing.

IDOL THREATS

What is the stimulus to this proud hearted questioning? Jesus has threatened their culture; he has provoked change; they are blinded with jealousy; they are frothing with a pseudo-righteous desire to protect "the way things are done around here." "Their way" has become an idol in their hearts.

This is us. We do this. We do this a lot. When the threat of change comes knocking on our door, our first and seemingly natural response is often to give ourselves the benefit of the doubt, even against Scripture, protecting our own personal culture at any cost. If we don't want to change, we shield ourselves to preserve our way; we can demonize the change agent. We fixate on minutia in order to bolster a case against the change agent. We scheme in private to empower our case against the change agent. We lie to ourselves in order to secure our case against the change agent. Jesus himself, working in the world, fell victim to this dark behavioral pattern. So also those who represent him will face similar resistance when the progressive work of the Lord and his Word threatens the status quo.

This happens when the new guy on the job is praised for his productivity, challenging existing culture in the workplace by his results. This happens when pastors feel threatened by new ideas from the congregation. This happens when congregations feel threatened by new possibilities from pastors. This happens when existing church members feel threatened by new church members with fresh perspectives, or emerging youth with radical ideas. This happens when we read Scripture and it challenges us, accuses us, calls us to change, commissions us on new paths.

Change is inevitable, unavoidable, irresistible. Jesus, the great change agent, threatens our own personal culture, the way things are done in our hearts and in our lives, by the very nature of who and what he is. Embracing the change that he brings can be unavoidably difficult, but is for the best, for our best. Embracing the change that he brings is the only path to becoming the disciple that he has called us to become. Embracing the change that he brings to our personal culture empowers us to become spiritual change-agents to the culture around us as well.

LIFE APPLICATIONS:

1. What areas of the religious leaders' culture (the way things are done around here) were most challenged and threatened by Jesus?

_____

_____

_____

_____

_____

_____

_____

_____

2. What areas of your personal culture (the way things are done in your life) and social culture (The way things are done in the work place, in the family, in the church, etc.) are most challenged and threatened by Jesus and Scripture? When in conflict with something in Scripture, do you typically give yourself or the Bible the benefit of the doubt? Explain.

_____

_____

_____

_____

_____

_____

_____

_____

3. How does the social culture around you affect your personal culture? How does your personal culture affect the social culture around you?

_____

_____

_____

_____

_____

_____

_____

_____

4. The Pharisees demonstrated a destructive, but common, behavioral pattern in their resistance to change—demonization, nitpicking, scheming, and entrapment. How have you experienced this pattern in your life? What steps could you take to short-circuit this pattern in your own heart when threatened with change? How could you become more redemptive in your interactions with those whom you perhaps threaten with change?

_____

_____

_____

_____

_____

_____

_____

_____

_____

_____

10

Matthew 23:1-39

Then, Jesus spoke to the multitudes and to his disciples, saying: "The scribes and the Pharisees sit in Moses' seat. Therefore, whatever they tell you to observe, that observe and do, but do not do according to their works; for they say, and do not do. For they bind heavy burdens, hard to bear, and lay them on men's shoulders; but they themselves will not move them with one of their fingers. But all their works they do to be seen by men. They make their phylacteries broad and enlarge the borders of their garments. They love the best places at feasts, the best seats in the synagogues, greetings in the marketplaces, and to be called by men, 'Rabbi, Rabbi.' But you, do not be called 'Rabbi'; for one is your Teacher, the Christ, and you are all brethren. Do not call anyone on earth your father; for one is your Father, he who is in heaven. And do not be called teachers; for one is your Teacher, the Christ. But he who is greatest among you shall be your servant. And whoever exalts himself will be humbled, and he who humbles himself will be exalted.

"But woe to you, scribes and Pharisees, hypocrites! For you shut up the kingdom of heaven against men; for you neither go in yourselves, nor do you allow those who are entering to go in. Woe to you, scribes and Pharisees, hypocrites! For you devour widows' houses, and for a pretense make long prayers. Therefore, you will receive greater condemnation.

"Woe to you, scribes and Pharisees, hypocrites! For you travel land and sea to win one proselyte, and when he is won, you make him twice as much a son of hell as yourselves.

"Woe to you, blind guides, who say, 'Whoever swears by the temple, it is nothing; but whoever swears by the gold of the temple, he is obliged to perform it.' Fools and blind! For which is greater, the gold or the temple that sanctifies the gold? And, 'Whoever swears by the altar, it is nothing; but whoever swears by the gift that is on it, he is obliged to perform it.' Fools and blind! For which is greater, the gift or the altar that sanctifies the gift? Therefore, he who swears by the altar, swears by it and by all things on it. He who swears by the temple, swears by it and by him who dwells in it. And he who swears by heaven, swears by the throne of God and by him who sits on it.

"Woe to you, scribes and Pharisees, hypocrites! For you pay tithe of mint and anise and cumin, and have neglected the weightier matters of the law: justice and mercy and faith. These you ought to have done, without leaving the others undone. Blind guides, who strain out a gnat and swallow a camel!

"Woe to you, scribes and Pharisees, hypocrites! For you cleanse the outside of the cup and dish, but inside they are full of extortion and self-indulgence. Blind Pharisee, first cleanse the inside of the cup and dish, that the outside of them may be clean also.

"Woe to you, scribes and Pharisees, hypocrites! For you are like whitewashed tombs which indeed appear beautiful outwardly, but inside are full of dead men's bones and all uncleanness. Even so you also outwardly appear righteous to men, but inside you are full of hypocrisy and lawlessness.

"Woe to you, scribes and Pharisees, hypocrites! Because you build the tombs of the prophets and adorn the monuments of the righteous, and say, 'If we had lived in the days of our fathers, we would not have been partakers with them in the blood of the prophets.'

"Therefore, you are witnesses against yourselves that you are sons of those who murdered the prophets. Fill up, then, the measure of your fathers' guilt. Serpents, brood of vipers! How can you escape the condemnation of hell?

"O Jerusalem, Jerusalem, the one who kills the prophets and stones those who are sent to her! How often I wanted to gather your children together, as a hen gathers her chicks under her wings, but you were not willing! See! Your house is left to you desolate; for I say to you, you shall see me no more till you say, 'Blessed is he who comes in the name of the LORD!'"

HYPOCRICY

On the heels of a coordinated attack against him by various types of religious leaders in Matthew 22, Jesus turns in chapter 23 to unleash a tirade of accusation against them. As we read, it seems that few things bring Christ to his boiling point faster than *hypocrisy*. The popular picture of the hypocrite is the gaudy and corrupt televangelist, or the legalistic religious fanatic whose Sunday mornings are spent voicing loud attention-getting "Hallelujahs" in a short hiatus from wife beating, child abuse and infidelity. Indeed, given Jesus' depiction of the religious leaders of his day, these would be good examples, but hypocrisy is more insidious than that, lurking close to the heart in almost every human interaction.

The word *hypocrisy*, or *hypocrite* comes from the Greek word meaning *play actor*—a phony. Through Jesus' description of these leaders' particular demonstrations of hypocrisy—broad phylacteries,[i] enlarged garment borders, veggie garden tithes, lawyered-up oaths, and the like—we see the true and ugly heart of hypocrisy—the false face, incongruity of profession and action. As Jesus put it, "They say and do not." This is the basic attribute of a hypocrite—professing one thing while doing another. It can be summed up in the motto, *Do as I say, not as I do.*

Jesus isolates the motive of hypocrisy—people love to be seen by others, praised by others, admired by others. This desire is common to us all; we all love to be noticed for the good we do. When we do what we do solely to gain the admiration of men, however, we are laying the groundwork of hypocrisy. Once this groundwork is laid, then it has to be maintained, because as soon as our actual behavior threatens to rob us of admiration and benefits, we put up a facade to protect that admiration, to preserve those benefits.

Hypocrisy is born in subtlety. It begins with a slight shift in motive away from "Doing the right thing," "Being a blessing to others," and "Pleasing God," toward, "Being regarded," "Being praised," and "Being rewarded." Once we are no longer focused on being clean, so much as looking clean, we set up a scenario that permits a steady disintegration of behavior behind a never changing facade of righteousness, goodness, selflessness, or the like.

We are on our way to becoming like the Pharisees when we strive for praise, when our hearts swell with pride to hear the words, "Pastor," "Doctor," or "wonderful," "talented," or even "good." We are like the Pharisee when we win people to the name of Christ and set ourselves over them as indispensible gateways to God, more concerned that they be like us, than that they be like Jesus. We are like the Pharisees when we live for the externals rather than internals, when we care more about performance than attitude. We are like them when our capacity for self-justification grows, excusing our greed and dishonesty and immorality, even crafting convoluted loopholes in Scripture for our behavior. When we become like the Pharisees, true love and mercy are the first things to fade.

NOTORIETY

No matter how big or small, how seemingly noble, we all have a desire to be recognized. The need for notoriety is a strong motivating force and comes standard with us all. This is not always a bad thing; we need to live in community to survive and need to cooperate with our community to be in community. The question is, "What lies are we willing to project about ourselves to have community acceptance?" Whose acceptance matters most—God's or man's? From the rock star, to the pastor, to the parking attendant— hypocrisy emerges in us when our desire for praise, or our need to be accepted and noticed takes over, or outweighs the desire to do the right thing for the right reason.

The Pharisees present us some extreme examples, indeed, and I'm sure, if we tried, we could come up with a handful of modern examples to rival their level of hypocrisy, but this would be to ignore the seed of it in our own hearts—the pride of admiration and the subtle shift in motivation that it can bring.

We are all guilty of this in some measure. We all suffer from the same sick condition that desires the praise of men in some form or another. When I came to Christ, it was like I was able to look into the mirror of my heart and see its condition. I hated what I saw. I perceived that the life I'd been living, the music I had been writing, the goals I had set all had their motivation in garnering some sense of acceptance and notoriety from man. Even though man's recognition has never and can never satisfy this insatiable desire in every human heart, I searched blindly for it.

It wasn't until I found my acceptance and praise from the Lord that the need for the praise of man diminished. When I found my motivation in him, in pleasing him, I was relieved; I could finally stop trying to please people. Having the praise and the smile of God over my life was enough, it was healing, it was medication to my condition.

LIFE APPLICATIONS:

1. Can you share an instance in your life when you felt the love of notoriety take hold? How did that affect your behavior?

_____

_____

_____

_____

_____

_____

_____

_____

_____

_____

2. What do you think motivates you to seek community approval? Do you ever present a false face to achieve and/or protect this approval? Explain.

_____

_____

_____

_____

_____

_____

_____

_____

_____

_____

3. Can you describe a time in your life when your sense of acceptance by God overshadowed your need for human acceptance?

_____

_____

_____

_____

_____

_____

_____

_____

_____

_____

11

MATTHEW 24 SUITE

Matthew 24:1-14, 29-31, 42-51

Then, Jesus went out and departed from the temple, and his disciples came up to show him the buildings of the temple. And Jesus said to them, "Do you not see all these things? Assuredly, I say to you, not one stone shall be left here upon another, that shall not be thrown down."

Now as he sat on the Mount of Olives, the disciples came to him privately, saying, "Tell us, when will these things be? And what will be the sign of your coming, and of the end of the age?"

And Jesus answered and said to them: "Take heed that no one deceives you. For many will come in my name, saying, 'I am the Christ,' and will deceive many. And you will hear of wars and rumors of wars. See that you are not troubled; for all these things must come to pass, but the end is not yet. For nation will rise against nation, and kingdom against kingdom. And there will be famines, pestilences, and earthquakes in various places. All these are the beginning of sorrows.

"Then, they will deliver you up to tribulation and kill you, and you will be hated by all nations for my name's sake. And then many will be offended, will betray one another, and will hate one another. Then, many false prophets will rise up and deceive many. And because lawlessness will abound, the love of many will grow cold. But he who endures to the end shall be saved. And this gospel of the kingdom will be preached in all the world as a witness to all the nations, and then the end will come.

Immediately after the tribulation of those days the sun will be darkened, and the moon will not give its light; the stars will fall from heaven, and the powers of the heavens will be shaken. Then, the sign of the Son of Man will appear in heaven, and then all the tribes of the earth will mourn, and they will see the Son of Man coming on the clouds of heaven with power and great glory. And he will send his angels with a great sound of a trumpet, and they will gather together his elect from the four winds, from one end of heaven to the other.

Watch therefore, for you do not know what hour your Lord is coming. But know this, that if the master of the house had known what hour the thief would come, he would have watched and not allowed his house to be broken into. Therefore, you also be ready, for the Son of Man is coming at an hour you do not expect.

Who then is a faithful and wise servant, whom his master made ruler over his household, to give them food in due season? Blessed is that servant whom his master, when he comes, will find so doing. Assuredly, I say to you that he will make him ruler over all his goods. But if that evil servant says in his heart, 'my master is delaying his coming,' and begins to beat his fellow servants, and to eat and drink with the drunkards, the master of that servant will come on a day when he is not looking for him and at an hour that he is not aware of, and will cut him in two and appoint him his portion with the hypocrites. There shall be weeping and gnashing of teeth."

THE SONG

The song for Matthew 24 was not in the SAVIOR Musical when I first wrote it. Later, while my wife and I were living in Nashville, TN, we took up the task of revising the musical as a whole for studio recording. The revision process took about a year. Every original song was scrutinized— tweaked, re-written, left alone, or pitched; some entirely new songs, like the "Matthew 24 Suite" were added. During this process, I read carefully through the gospels to see if anything crucial from the Passion Week had been neglected. When I read through the Matthew 24 section, I knew we had to add it;

Christ's message about the end times was too important to leave out.

When I thought of this prophecy as a song, I saw it in two parts: dark & light, or judgment & salvation. Most of Christ's prophecy is pretty grim. Jesus gives his disciples a heavy list of events that would take place on earth—deception, wars, famine, earthquakes, pestilence. As if these weren't bad enough, he tells them that they are just "the beginning of sorrows." There will be yet more to come—tribulation, martyrdom, false prophets, mass deception and a great falling away of the church. This first part is by far one of the darkest prophesies in the Bible, but the second part (v.31) is much brighter—the coming of the Son.

THE WHAT

These days, there is no little contradictory opinion and open debate regarding the second coming of Christ, or what is considered by some to be the rapture of the church; much of this struggle is over the specific meaning of Matthew 24 as it relates to both the A.D. 70 destruction of Jerusalem, clearly in view in at least part of this prophecy, and the second coming of Jesus, which many suggest is also clearly in view in other parts of this prophecy. Rather than talking about the nature of prophecy and fulfillment, or the *when*, the *why* and the *how* of the Lord's coming, I'd like to focus most of our attention on the *what* in Matthew 24. *What* is Christ's message to us in light of these impending events? *What* are appropriate applications of that message.

THREE BIG QUESTIONS

After giving his disciples a description of the destruction of Jerusalem—not a stone left atop another—Jesus walks out of the temple for the last time to go sit on the Mount of Olives, the perfect spot for viewing Jerusalem. Some of the disciples come to him privately to ask him three big questions: 1. When will these things be? 2. What will be the sign of your coming? 3. What will be the sign of the end of the age?

Jesus' answer to these questions focuses on many signs which are less than specific, signs that are observable throughout human history, ebbing and flowing, but seeming in his vision to eventually reach an apex of such severity that even the most faithful need fear for their capacity to stand in the midst of it. The gospel will be shared the world over, but darkness and tribulation will ensue.

THE WISE AND EVIL SERVANT

In the midst of all this, what is Jesus' concern? What is Jesus' advice? Time charts? Figuring out the date of his return? Selling everything and sitting in a field to wait? Forgetting about any of it and living only for the moment? No. Jesus advises wisdom manifested in a dedication to the work of the Lord, regardless of the circumstances, or how long it takes for him to return. The Lord may have gone, but his disciples should live as if they were expecting his return. They should keep busy in the work he has commanded during his absence, lest they be taken unawares by his return, delinquent in the task.

Then, Jesus describes two types of servants—*wise* and *evil*. Each regards himself as the servant of the Lord, but only one keeps busy with the task. Both, no doubt, begin the wait with eager expectation, but, sooner or later, the laziness or selfishness or immorality or dishonesty of the one seems to go unpunished; the master has not popped up to accuse. So, he gets the idea, little by little, that he can live any way he wants. In the parable, the Lord returns to this evil servant as his judge.

As I write this, my wife and I are expecting company. Soon, we will begin preparing for their arrival, getting our house in order. We will go shopping, cook food, clean the house, wash ourselves and busy ourselves with a myriad of little preparations right up to the moment they arrive. If we prepare this way for our friends, how much more diligently should we prepare for the coming of our Lord—even if his coming is delayed.

Imagine the scene if we didn't prepare, if we got sidetracked with our own stuff. It would be weird. "O, hey, sorry about the messy house," and, "I know we said we'd have dinner ready, but we didn't prepare anything, or go shopping." Imagine this same scene if our visitor were a senator, the President, or a foreign king... the scandal and shame would be monumental, the offense incalculable. How much more seriously should we take the preparation for our coming Lord and SAVIOR?

I said at first that I saw in Jesus' prophecy in Matthew 24 both dark & light—dark in the disasters leading to his coming and light in his coming. So far, however, we've spoken of his coming in darkness and fearful foreboding. Where is the light? The light comes to the faithful servant who fulfills his master's commission, who is found waiting and watching, setting his hopes on his master's return. We might wonder what the spiritual equivalent would be to the blessing bestowed upon the wise servant in the parable, but, here, the master gives him rule and sustenance for a lifetime.

Jesus gives this shocking prophecy of darkness unleashed and what is his application of it to life? Be prepared for his coming by continuing to do the work he has assigned you until the end. Watch and wait... never forget that he's coming.

LIFE APPLICATIONS:

1. How does reading Jesus' description of the time leading up to his return make you feel?

_____

_____

_____

_____

_____

_____

_____

_____

_____

_____

2. If Jesus returned today, explain the ways you might be regarded as either, or both, a wise servant and/or an evil servant.

_____

_____

_____

_____

_____

_____

_____

_____

_____

3. Name three things you could do immediately to be a wiser servant. Be specific.

_____

_____

_____

_____

_____

_____

_____

_____

_____

_____

12

30 SILVER COINS

John 12:1-8

Six days before the Passover, Jesus came to Bethany, where Lazarus was who had been dead, whom he had raised from the dead. There they made him a supper; and Martha served, but Lazarus was one of those who sat at the table with him. Then, Mary took a pound of very costly oil of spikenard, anointed the feet of Jesus, and wiped his feet with her hair. And the house was filled with the fragrance of the oil.

But one of his disciples, Judas Iscariot, Simon's *son*, who would betray him, said, "Why was this fragrant oil not sold for three hundred denarii and given to the poor?" This he said, not that he cared for the poor, but because he was a thief, and had the moneybox; and he used to take what was put in it.

But Jesus said, "Leave her alone; she has kept this for the day of my burial. For the poor you have with you always, but me you do not have always."

Matthew 26:12-16

For in pouring this fragrant oil on my body, she did *it* for my burial. Assuredly, I say to you, wherever this gospel is preached in the whole world, what this woman has done will also be told as a memorial to her."

Then, Judas, one of the twelve, went to the chief priests and said, "What are you willing to give me if I hand him over to you?" And they counted out to him thirty pieces of silver. So from that time, he sought opportunity to betray him.

JUDAS AND MARY

The gospels of Matthew and John allow us to peer into a room where Jesus is dinning with his disciples. Here, we see two characters—Mary and Judas. They couldn't be any more different.

Mary, forgiven of many sins, cleansed of many devils, is dining with Jesus and her brother, Lazarus, whom Jesus has just raised from the dead. We see a woman overflowing with thanksgiving, praise and adoration for her Lord, who had performed great miracles in her life. To say she is appreciative would be a dramatic understatement—she embodies the idea that who is forgiven much, loves much. (Luke 7:47)

She takes a jar of uber-expensive ointment and anoints the Lord with it, even wiping his feet with her hair! This may sound gross and uncomfortable to us, but in their culture this was a great honor. Mary gave all she could, not only the costly ointment, but her abounding love, her respect, even her dignity. Her overwhelming love for the Lord was so much that she didn't care about what others would say, or think. This is true worship.

Nearby, we see Judas—a thieving "accountant" who found no difficulty in stealing from the Lord's treasury. He was a man living a double life, holding the appearance of an uncompromising disciple of Jesus, while cultivating an inner life full of avarice and greed, serving Christ for his own gain. The gospel's contrast with Mary exposes the depth of his corruption.

For Judas, Lazarus's presence with them, a living testimony of Jesus' power and authority, has no lasting internal impact. Mary glorifies the Lord in her thankful act of worship for raising her brother from the dead, but Judas' covetous heart sees none of this; he is angry. He cloaks his perturbed greed with pious concerns for the poor, but he saw Mary's act of worship as a missed opportunity for stolen gain. Jesus rebukes Judas for his pseudo-spiritual protests and Judas comes, I believe, to his heart's breaking point with Jesus. Judas is silenced, but, in his mind, he is screaming. He is rebuked in front of his friends and fellow disciples and is, no doubt, humiliated. The greed of Judas' heart collides head-on with Jesus' ultimate intentions for coming into this world.

Jesus was, likely, early on, Judas' path to self-fulfillment, but when Jesus disappoints and humiliates him, he takes matters into his own hands. Perhaps, he means to salvage Jesus' messiahship, and his own rise to power with him, by forcing him into a lethal confrontation with both the Romans and the Jewish leaders. Perhaps, he merely betrays Jesus to get more money. Either way, the price of Judas' soul ends up being the thirty pieces of silver for which he turns Jesus over to his enemies, which, oddly enough, was the going rate for a slave. Judas sells himself into slavery to his own sin for 30 pieces of silver.

THE MARY AND JUDAS WITHIN

When following Jesus doesn't live up to our preconceived expectations, when the Lord doesn't deliver all that *we* want, we can be tempted to react like Judas and walk away from him. When I gave my life to Christ, the rest of the guys in our band, *The Trees,* soon followed. It was Dave, Rich, Brian, and myself. Rich and Brian's commitment to Christ seemed reluctant, however. They were willing to go to church, pray and even read their Bibles, as long as nothing changed with their plans of "making it" with our music.

Unlike Rich, Brian was more vocal about his resistance to change. I remember him telling me one night, "I don't want to follow God because he's going to make me do what I don't want to do." I naively said, "Why would he do that?" Knowing what I know now, however, I understand why he was struggling. Even after making a commitment to Christ, there came a point when Brian realized that he could no longer get what he wanted for his life and follow Jesus at the same time; he had some hard decisions to make.

The human response to this fundamental conflict is what makes Judas and Mary so different. Mary gave all she could, without care of the cost; Judas took all he could without care of the consequence. He lived a double life, keeping up appearances as a disciple, while stealing and plotting. When he could no longer get what he wanted, he walked away. I am not labeling any of my friends "Judas," but I learned a hard lesson in those days. I had to check my own personal motive, my preconceived ideas of God and the expectations that I put on Jesus. Even agendas that I may have about the benefits of following him need inspection, or, one day I might walk away as well.

The strife witnessed at the dinner table in John 12 between Mary and Judas reflects our own internal struggle. Within all of us, there is a Mary that wants to worship and a Judas who wants only for himself. They oppose each other. It's spirit versus flesh. Mary's actions are praised by Jesus; he is honored when we pour out our love and gratitude to God, from a thankful and selfless heart of worship.

LIFE APPLICATIONS:

1. Do you have any sense of this internal struggle between the selfless worshiper and the selfish sinner in relation to Christ? Can you describe the nature of this struggle in your own life?

_____

_____

_____

_____

_____

_____

_____

_____

_____

_____

2. What would you consider to be a "deal breaker" in your relationship with Christ? Do you fear that continuing to serve Christ will remove or add something seemingly intolerable to your life? What would an intolerable situation look like for you? How do you imagine you would respond?

_____

_____

_____

_____

_____

_____

_____

_____

_____

3. Can you describe areas in your life where you're living a double standard, keeping up appearances in one way, while living selfishly in another?

_____

_____

_____

_____

_____

_____

_____

_____

_____

4. Have you ever had a spiritual experience with Christ that was so moving that it helps you to understand Mary's gratitude and sacrificial worship? Can you share it?

_____

_____

_____

_____

_____

_____

_____

_____

_____

_____

13

IF YOU WILL BELIEVE

John 12:44-50

Then, Jesus cried out and said, "He who believes in me, believes not in me but in him who sent me. And he who sees me sees him who sent me. I have come as a light into the world, that whoever believes in me should not abide in darkness. And if anyone hears my words and does not believe, I do not judge him; for I did not come to judge the world but to save the world.

He who rejects me, and does not receive my words, has that which judges him—the word that I have spoken will judge him in the last day. For I have not spoken on my own authority; but the Father who sent me gave me a command, what I should say and what I should speak. And I know that his command is everlasting life. Therefore, whatever I speak, just as the Father has told me, so I speak."

BELIEF IN BELIEVING

When we talk about belief in God, it is important to define our terms. For instance, if I were to ask you if you believe in God, you would, perhaps, say, "Yes." The question is, however, what do you mean by your *yes*, what do you mean by *belief?* To some, belief in God simply means a mental assent, an acknowledgment of a philosophy, a basic acceptance in the possible existence of God. In fact, most people in the world today affirm that they believe in God, but perhaps what many are saying is that they agree with the theoretical idea of a God and, therefore, retain the concept of a God in their minds.

I BELIEVE IN GOD

Growing up, I had a belief in God. I was raised in the Catholic Church; I went to Catholic grade schools. Throughout my teenage years and into my early twenties, however, I wasn't living as any kind of Christian. The night Dave and Shelby came to our band rehearsal and began to talk about how Christ had changed their lives and how we could live in close relationship with God, I began to think about what I truly believed. Growing up, I had heard some of what they were saying, but not like this. I thought I agreed with them; I tried to agree with them, but I could sense in myself the contradiction; my lifestyle did not support my claim.

It wasn't that I felt guilty for failing to keep religious rules and regulations, but I knew I didn't have any real relationship with God; I didn't concern myself with him, or any potential plan he might have for me. I certainly didn't have the joy and peace that I could see in the lives of Dave and Shelby. What they had was real. It exposed to my own heart that my confidence and the "got-it-all-together-ness" of my public persona was a facade. Inside, I was lonely, angry and broken. I had been using drugs, alcohol and sex as a way to self-soothe, to desensitize, to fight off my growing depression. The effects of my sinful life were taking their toll on me, and I knew it.

That night at rehearsal, a little light broke into my darkness. In Dave and Shelby, I could see sincere love, true joy and a real and supernatural peace through the Spirit of Jesus living through them. This was the moment when I started to understand what it meant to truly believe.

BELIEVING AND KEEPING

In John 12, Jesus gives his very own definition of *belief* and it goes well beyond mental assent. According to Jesus, to *believe* in him is to believe that the Father sent him as a light into a dark world. Those that have this kind of belief in Christ will not live in darkness, but in his light. Christ uses the term light to describe the illumination of truth in the life of a believer. His truth is his Word and his Word become a light in our life, revealing Jesus to us and lighting the paths of our lives. Jesus uses the same description of *belief* in the famous John 3:16 passage:

> "God so loved the world that he gave his only begotten son, that whoever *believes* in him should not perish, but have everlasting life. For God did not send his son into the world to condemn the world, but that the world through him might be saved.
>
> He who *believes* in him is not condemned; but he who does not *believe* is condemned already, because he has not believed in the name of the only begotten son of God. And this is the condemnation, that the light has come into the world, and men loved darkness rather than light, because their deeds were evil. For everyone practicing evil hates the light and does not come to the light, lest his deeds should be exposed. But he who does the truth comes to the light, that his deeds may be clearly seen, that they have been done in God." (John 3:16-21)

To Jesus, belief isn't just the acknowledgement of facts concerning the existence of God, or of the deity of Christ; true belief is lived out. Belief changes what you do and how you think.

Think about it this way; we naturally live by our beliefs. In the same way that I set my alarm because I believe that the sun will rise tomorrow, my actions declare what I truly believe. If I believe that a bridge will hold me up, I demonstrate this by walking across it confidently when I come to it. If I truly believe in God, I will naturally believe what he says; I'll obey his Word; I'll even seek him out. Why wouldn't I? What I believe about God is manifested in how I live and to Jesus, *believing* and *obeying* are synonymous. He's right, they can't be separated.

If we truly believe in him, then we will believe what he has said of himself: He has come as a light of truth. He has come as a SAVIOR into the world to deliver us from the bondage of sin and death. If we truly believe in him, then we will follow his commands and live out his call to us, becoming his disciples. The proof, or charade, of our professions concerning him is discovered in our actions. So, if you say you believe in God, find out if your actions, if your life, is lining up with your profession.

LIFE APPLICATIONS:

1. Describe some practical ways in which your general beliefs about reality are reflected in your actions.

_____

_____

_____

_____

_____

_____

_____

_____

_____

_____

2. List some ways that your beliefs in God do line up and do not line up with your lifestyle.

_____

_____

_____

_____

_____

_____

_____

_____

_____

_____

3. How do your Bible study habits relate to your claims regarding Scripture as God's Word?

_____

_____

_____

_____

_____

_____

_____

_____

_____

4. Do the claims of Jesus about himself affect the choices that you make day to day? Do you consciously seek to keep his commands? Explain.

_____

_____

_____

_____

_____

_____

_____

_____

_____

14

THE LAST SUPPER

Matthew 26:20-22; 26-29

When evening had come, he sat down with the twelve. Now as they were eating, he said, "Assuredly, I say to you, one of you will betray me."

And they were exceedingly sorrowful, and each of them began to say to him, "Lord, is it I?"

And as they were eating, Jesus took bread, blessed and broke it, and gave it to the disciples and said, "Take, eat; this is my body."

Then, he took the cup, and gave thanks, and gave it to them, saying, "Drink from it, all of you. For this is my blood of the new covenant, which is shed for many for the remission of sins. But I say to you, I will not drink of this fruit of the vine from now on until that day when I drink it new with you in my father's kingdom."

John 13:2-5; 12-17; 34-35

And supper being ended, the devil having already put it into the heart of Judas Iscariot, Simon's son, to betray him, Jesus, knowing that the Father had given all things into his hands, and that he had come from God and was going to God, rose from supper and laid aside his garments, took a towel and girded himself. After that, he poured water into a basin and began to wash the disciples' feet, and to wipe them with the towel with which he was girded. Then, he came to Simon Peter. And Peter said to him, "Lord, are you washing my feet?"

Jesus answered and said to him, "What I am doing you do not understand now, but you will know after this."

So when he had washed their feet, taken his garments, and sat down again, he said to them, "Do you know what I have done to you? You call me Teacher and Lord, and you say well, for so I am. If I then, your Lord and Teacher, have washed your feet, you also ought to wash one another's feet. For I have given you an example that you should do as I have done to you. Most assuredly, I say to you, a servant is not greater than his master; nor is he who is sent greater than he who sent him. If you know these things, blessed are you if you do them."

Jesus said, "A new commandment I give to you, that you love one another; as I have loved you, that you also love one another. By this all will know that you are my disciples, if you have love for one another."

COMMUNION

When I was a boy, my father would take me to Catholic mass. The high point of the mass is the taking of communion. To this impatient young man, communion was that point in the service when we walked up to the front of the church and received a bland tasting round wafer from the priest, ate it, then sat down again. It had great significance to me; it meant mass was almost over. *Yaaaaahoooo!!*

During communion, I remember joining a long processional of people in a slow walk up to the front of the church, standing in front of the priest, stretching out my little hands, as he took a wafer out of a golden bowl and placed it into my cupped palms. Then in a monotone voice, he'd intone, "Body of Christ." I had no idea what that meant. I just ate the wafer and sat back down. That was communion to me, but Jesus has more than this in mind when he says in Luke 22:19, "Do this in remembrance of me."

PASSOVER

Our communion didn't originate in a church building, but in Egypt with a Jewish supper called Passover. It commemorates the story of the Exodus, in which the ancient Israelites were freed from slavery in Egypt and recalls the last of the ten plagues. That was the night, thousands of years ago, when the angel of death visited every home in Egypt, killing the eldest son, harmlessly *passing-over* only those households who painted their doorway with the blood of a sacrificial lamb. Hence, *"Passover."*

In our passage, Jesus celebrates the Passover as his last meal with his 12 disciples. (Matthew 26:17ff) During the meal, he fills an already symbol-rich celebration with powerful new meaning. He is the Lamb of God, whose body will be broken and whose blood will be shed to mark those who will be *passed-over* and saved from eternal death. He established the Passover meal as a renewed celebration of a new *covenant*, secured through his blood.

A NEW COVENANT

A covenant is a pact sworn before a judging God or gods; this God (or gods) is believed to hold each to their oaths in the pact. Covenants were commonly initiated through symbolic acts—like the shed blood of a sacrificial animal—that represented the threat of death against those in the covenant. Often, the ingestion of the elements of a covenant initiation was an oath that said in essence, "If I don't keep my promises in this covenant, may God judge me."

In this final Passover meal, Jesus uses elements of that covenant initiation to symbolize a coming new covenant, sealed by the shed blood of the Son of God. The bread represents his broken body. The wine represents his shed blood. Our ingestion represents our promises of fidelity to him and to others in the covenant.

Ok, so back to our original question. What did Jesus mean when he said, "Do this in remembrance of me?" When we take communion, we are *"remembering"* that we are in a common-union with God and his people. We are *"remembering"* the gospel of Jesus, the SAVIOR, who came and gave his life as a sacrifice for our sins, establishing the long awaited new covenant of peace with God. (Jeremiah 31:31) We "remember" that we are freed from the slavery of sin and, by the blood of the lamb of God, eternal death will *pass us over*.

In the ancient world, *remembrance* was more than mental recollection, however, it also meant to actively keep covenant promises. In communion, we swear loyalty to Jesus and loyalty to others who swear loyalty to him, but we also promise fidelity to his commands… chief of which, he exemplifies after the meal—"love one another as I have loved you."

A NEW COMMANDMENT

The last words of a dying man are often some of his most important. These words, spoken at the last supper, are among Jesus' last. With the new covenant, came a new commandment—to love as Jesus loved. Love in the Bible is not some blanket acceptance of other people's crud, nor the cultivation of warm fuzzy feelings for another. Love was a determined course of action intended for another's good. Jesus wanted us to be known by our love. Those that follow Christ are to be earmarked as *people who love*. Knowing this, he gives a powerful object lesson, a great example to understand what this kind of love would look like. It is love in action. He washes their feet.

Travelers in the biblical world often had dirty, even dung-besmeared feet. It was the job of the lowest servant in the house to greet guests and wash this filth from them. Here, at the Last Supper, however, no disciple was willing to play such a role for the others. So, they sit reclining with their unwashed feet in each other's faces throughout the meal; how appetizing.

When dinner was over, Jesus, fully aware of who he was and what he was doing, (Re-read his resume in John above) took off his garment, wrapped a servant's towel around himself and proceeded to wash his disciples' feet. Having done so, he says, "I have given you an example that you should do as I have done to you." One of the things that strikes me most about this is that he even washes the feet of Judas, knowing that he would betray him. That's the kind of love Jesus was exemplifying for us.

This was a new commandment—a new, radical and counter-cultural demonstration of love. This new kind of Christ-like expression is a sacrificial, unconditional, humble, laying-down of-one's-life-for-others kind of love. It verifies that we belong to him; it is a witness to others that the spirit of Christ is in us.

This kind of selfless, Christ-like love was one of the first things I recognized from the day I walked into that small New England church with Dave and Shelby. In the weeks and months to follow, as I got to know the Christian community in Southern New England, I realized that this Christ-like love wasn't just bound to my church, or my denomination, but it was a common trait to all who loved and followed Christ. I remember how refreshingly different it was to witness. There was a true sense of selfless devotion that people shared for each other. It was endearing.

I wish that everyone who encounters the body of Christ could experience this love. Some churches struggle to show love to those on the outside, some on the outside struggle to perceive love in the church's message. Even so, Christ has called us to be a community known as *people who love*, people who intentionally act for the good of others. In this way, in this selflessly devoted and loving way, all who know us will encounter his love through us, and know that we belong to him.

LIFE APPLICATIONS:

1. Are you in a "covenant relationship" with God? Do you feel a common-union with other followers of Christ? Try to describe it.

_____

_____

_____

_____

_____

_____

_____

_____

_____

_____

2. How would you define love? How would you describe Jesus' love? How do these perceptions of love relate with your experiences with professing Christians?

_____

_____

_____

_____

_____

_____

_____

_____

_____

_____

3. What changes could you make in attitudes and actions to love others as Christ loves you?

_____

_____

_____

_____

_____

_____

_____

_____

_____

_____

4. Is there a Judas in your life to whom you struggle to show love? How could you change your heart toward him or her to adjust your actions to love like Jesus loved?

_____

_____

_____

_____

_____

_____

_____

_____

_____

_____

15

I'D DIE FOR YOU

Mark 14:27-31

Then, Jesus said to them, "All of you will be made to stumble because of me this night, for it is written:

'I will strike the shepherd, and the sheep will be scattered.'

"But after I have been raised, I will go before you to Galilee."

Peter said to him, "Even if all are made to stumble, yet I will not be."

Jesus said to him, "Assuredly, I say to you that today, even this night, before the rooster crows twice, you will deny me thrice."

But he spoke more vehemently, "If I have to die with you, I will not deny you!" And they all said likewise.

TOUGH KID

When I was in the 4th grade, my parents were in a custody dispute, and I ended up changing schools twice. It was also in 4th grade when my father enrolled me in a Catholic School for the first time. A few months later, when my mother gained custody, I was plucked out of that school and deposited into a different Catholic School. New schools, new religion. I was uncomfortable to say the least.

During that first day in the new Catholic school, it came to my attention that a certain young girl "liked me." (Not bad for the first day.) It also came to my knowledge, however, that a certain young boy "liked her," and therefore, *didn't* "like me."

The angry young man cornered me in the schoolyard during recess to expound on his feelings. His barrage of insults got the attention of the other kids and, soon, there was a crowd. I was not a little scared. I looked around at their eager faces, waiting for a fight to break out. Being the youngest of three brothers, fist fighting wasn't a foreign concept to me, but I had never been in a fight at school.

As the boy's insults grew worse, and the crowd grew bigger, my fear took over, and, before I knew it, I slugged him in the stomach. He doubled over, took a moment to catch his breath and, then, began to cry… loudly. Luckily, the schoolyard lady didn't see, and I didn't get in trouble. Instead, I got something else—praise.

Apparently, the angry young man was the class tough kid, and I had dethroned him. Soon, kids wanted to be my friend; they were nice to me and no one bothered me. This made me feel safe.

About halfway through the school year, my dad gained custody of me, took me out of that school and sent me back to the first Catholic school, closer to his house in Providence, Rhode Island. I lost my class tough kid status and was scared again. Soon, someone picked on me during lunch. So, during recess, I slugged him. I didn't have much of a repertoire back then, but I did have the same results—he doubled over and cried, and I became the "tough new kid," the alpha male... hear me roar. I was safe once again.

Being the tough kid, however, comes with its challenges. It meant that I would have to fight to maintain my title. I loved the hype and soon embraced the hype, believing I really was the tough kid… but I hated fighting. Looking back, I realize that maintaining that image was just my way of dealing with fear, a way to keep myself safe. By defending that image, however, I was not able to see and deal effectively with my real problem.

THE ROCK

We all have ideas of who we are. Some of us, like me, have grown up believing what other people have said about us, good or bad. We all have the capacity to believe that we're someone that we're not, and we tend to defend it. The Apostle Peter had some ideas about himself, too. He reveals them after the last supper.

Peter took pride in being the most committed of the disciples. Early on in their journey, Jesus changed his name from Simon to Peter, meaning, "Rock" (*Petros*). In his mind, Peter could never abandon the Lord. Surely, THE ROCK would remain faithful, even to death. This self-impression is so embedded in him that he not only refutes the prophecy that all will scatter like sheep, but believes that Jesus is wrong and in need of correction. It's as if Peter is saying, "Sorry, Jesus. You're off on this one. Me, THE ROCK, deny you? Not a chance." Even Jesus' more specific prediction of Peter's failure leaves him undaunted. Peter, no doubt, puts great stake in Jesus' opinion of him and, in order to protect this image, he defends himself, putting unwarranted and overblown confidence in his own strength.

Lest we're too hard on Peter, we should realize that Peter's problem is a human problem; Peter's problem is our problem; Peter's problem is my problem. In essence, Peter hears some news about himself that he doesn't want to hear; he takes it as criticism and becomes defensive. Like Peter, we often become defensive, even irate, when criticized. Criticism can be right or wrong, constructive, or deconstructive, but criticism in general has the ability to reveal personal weakness that we may not see... weakness that we may not want to see.

How we respond to critical opinions about ourselves often reveals more about us than about the issue at hand. Criticism can reveal insecurities and can play off past hurts. It can touch a wound, causing overblown responses. Our fears can cause us to misinterpret criticism from others and to misapply its significance for our life.

Jesus' prediction that he would deny the Lord, is interpreted by Peter to mean that he is weak, timid, vulnerable. It is an insult to Peter's very devotion to his master. This "accusation" is too hard to take. He's *special* after all, he's been *special* to Jesus all this time, and he'll prove it. Though *all* fall away, surely THE ROCK will stand.

This, however, isn't Godly confidence, but selfish pride. Perhaps, his reaction is overcompensation for something he may already know about himself—a possible Shakespearean "he-doth-protest-too-much-methinks," moment.

Interestingly enough, Peter's denial of the Lord begins with his denial of his denial of the Lord. He cannot hear such condemning assessments of his devotion to a master whose prophetic power he has already begun to question because it demeans him personally, especially, he imagines, in Jesus' eyes. After all, no one wants to look bad in front of the coach.

What doesn't occur to Peter, however is that having weakness in one area doesn't mean that he is a complete and utter failure overall. Here his refusal to face his own weakness sets him up for a potential faith-destroying fall. His inability to allow Jesus to expose his failings is a bigger problem than the supposed failings themselves; the first step to recovery is admitting you have a problem.

So, how should Peter have responded?

To start, he may have done well not to rebuke Jesus... always a bad place to begin.

Second, proper response to criticism must come initially from proper interpretation of criticism. We have to rightly understand the truth of what is actually being said as opposed to what we think is being said. This means not allowing our emotions to come first, distorting the truth.

We have to be able to properly weigh criticism. Our tendency to see our overall worth reflected in the eyes of those who matter most to us, can leave us incapable of hearing a criticism for what it actually is, rather than emotionally blowing it up in our hearts into a wholesale condemnation. If you are married, this will likely make perfect sense to you. A particular criticism from one may seem little more than a sunspot, while the same criticism from another feels like a total eclipse.

We are loved immeasurably by God, but we are not special cases... ever. No one is above reproach. Rather than living in a self-protective bubble, unable, or unwilling, to hear negative commentary, we must come to terms with our true selves. Just as you can't see the back of your own head without a mirror, so, criticism can expose certain areas of weakness to your own heart. Therefore, the next time you're tempted to grow defensive over some criticism, try to remember that it can work for your own good if you'll allow it. Consider the source and think about what is actually being said, and, before you become too defensive, stop to ask yourself the question, "What am I defending?"

LIFE APPLICATIONS:

1. How do you tend to respond to criticism? Why? How might you make better use of even painful criticism. Do you find that you receive criticism differently from different people? Why do you think this is?

_____

_____

_____

_____

_____

_____

_____

_____

_____

_____

2. In what particular areas of your life do you find it hard to receive criticism? Is there a *special* investment, or a *special* pride that you have in that area? Is there a particular self-image that you are defending? Explain.

_____

_____

_____

_____

_____

_____

_____

_____

_____

3. Does accepting criticism in one area make you feel like a wholesale failure? What do you imagine is happening inside you to make you feel this way? What would help to give you a better perspective in that moment?

_____

_____

_____

_____

_____

_____

_____

_____

_____

_____

4. While you cannot control how criticism comes to you, do you imagine that there is a way to deliver criticism to others that might make its acceptance easier for them? Explain.

_____

_____

_____

_____

_____

_____

_____

_____

_____

16

FATHER

Mark 14:32-33

Then, they came to a place called Gethsemane; and he said to his disciples, "Sit here while I pray." And he took Peter, James, and John with him, and he began to be troubled and deeply distressed.

John 17:1-11; 20-23

After Jesus said this, he looked toward heaven and prayed: "Father, the time has come. Glorify your son, that your son also may glorify you, as you have given him authority over all flesh, that he should give eternal life to as many as you have given him. And this is eternal life, that they may know you, the only true God, and Jesus Christ whom you have sent. I have glorified you on the earth. I have finished the work which you have given me to do. And now, O Father, glorify me together with yourself, with the glory which I had with you before the world was.

I have manifested your name to the men whom you have given me out of the world. They were yours, you gave them to me, and they have kept your word. Now they have known that all things which you have given me are from you. For I have given to them the words which you have given me; and they have received them, and have known surely that I came forth from you; and they have believed that you sent me.

I pray for them. I do not pray for the world but for those whom you have given me, for they are yours. And all mine are yours, and yours are mine, and I am glorified in them. Now I am no longer in the world, but these are in the world, and I come to you. Holy Father, keep through your name those whom you have given me, that they may be one as we are.

I do not pray for these alone, but also for those who will believe in me through their word; that they all may be one, as you, Father, are in me, and I in you; that they also may be one in us, that the world may believe that you sent me. And the glory which you gave me I have given them, that they may be one just as we are one: I in them, and you in me; that they may be made perfect in one, and that the world may know that you have sent me, and have loved them as you have loved me. NIV

Luke 22:39-44

On reaching the place (the Garden of Gethsemane), he said to them, "Pray that you will not fall into temptation." He withdrew about a stone's throw beyond them, knelt down and prayed, "Father, if you are willing, take this cup from me; yet not my will, but yours be done." An angel from heaven appeared to him and strengthened him. And being in anguish, he prayed more earnestly, and his sweat was as it were great drops of blood falling to the ground. NIV

THE FREYTAG PYRAMID

During the 1800's, German playwright and novelist Gustav Freytag invented what is called The Freytag Pyramid. It was a way to structure a story into five parts. The middle parts are called: *rising action, climax* and *falling action. Rising action* is the great build up to an event. The *climax* is the act, or turning point in the story that causes change for the better or worse. *Falling action* is the result and sequence of consequences that follow the event. Up to this point of the gospel story, we have been witnessing what could be considered its "rising action," Jesus' submission to the will of the Father, here. in Gethsemane, we could envision as the "climax."

ON THE WAY TO THE GARDEN

After their last supper together, Jesus and the disciples go out into the night and walk to a garden called Gethsemane. John's gospel records the conversation he has with them: he tells them that the Holy Spirit will come to them after he is gone. He teaches them that as a branch they must stay connected to the vine in order to have life, so his disciples must stay connected to him. Then, he prays that they, and we, would be one with each other, one with him and one with the Father.

This is one of the greatest prayers recorded in the Bible. It sheds light on Christ's heart of intercession. In the SAVIOR album, we took great pains to capture musically and lyrically the mood and emotion of this prayer. It was hard to summarize such a long prayer in a single song, stretching as it does, over a few chapters in the gospel of John. His prayer turns into anguish. He knows the will of the Father. Horrific as it is, he surrenders to it. He prays, "Not my will, but yours be done."

NOT MY WILL, BUT YOURS BE DONE

Here is the "climax" of the gospel story. After Jesus fully gives over his will to the will of the Father, every other event becomes "falling action." Everything hinges on Jesus' willingness to sacrifice his life to fulfill the will of the Father. Christ knows both the terror of coming events and the enormity of their benefits. He knows he is about to take the burden and punishment for the past and present sins of the world, bringing salvation to man. He knows too, however, the wrath he is about to face; the temptation to avoid it is excruciating, so much so, Jesus sweats drops of blood.

The Garden of Gethsemane, where Christ was with his disciples that night, is an olive garden that sits at the foot of the Mount of Olives over an underground cave, containing an olive press. The word Gethsemane literally means, "oil press" in Aramaic. Shafts secured in the walls and weighed down with heavy stones were used to crush baskets filled with olives, crushing the oil out of them. Gethsemane is a fitting title for the place Christ knelt to pray, a great weight of anxiety pressing down upon him. Because of the love Jesus had for us, he surrendered, allowing the Gethsemane press of his Father's will, to crush his own. This is the place where, "Take this cup from me," becomes, "Not my will but yours be done."

SURRENDER

If we seek to follow Christ, eventually we come to our own Gethsemane—the place where we either say, "Father, not my will, but yours be done," or "Not your will, but mine be done."

I came to this place early in my Christian walk. It was a battle of wills. Was I going to choose my will for my life, or his? I had to decide. As stated, my music was a huge deal in my life, because at the time, it was my life; my whole identity was wrapped up in it; my whole sense of forward direction was built on it—*my* music, *my* plans, *my* life. I wanted people to tell me it was ok, or not ok to keep doing my thing. Nobody would. One pastor chuckled at my debate and asked, "Who are you arguing with? I'm not arguing with you." I wore people out with my internal wrangling. It was only when I finally wore myself out, however, that I truly understood that I was arguing with the Father's will. At long last, I submitted.

I had dinner with my band mate and writing partner, Rich, and told him that I couldn't fight God anymore, that I needed to give my music to Christ and exclusively write and play for him. Thinking, perhaps, that I was going to try to get him to switch the nature of the band, he told me that he couldn't do the same. "I'm not asking you to," I replied. Though I knew this would mean breaking up the band, I didn't change my decision.

I drove back to my house and walked into my dark living room, knelt down in front of the couch and prayed something like-*"Okay, Lord, here you go. You have everything now. I have nothing, but if you can use nothing, then here you go; here's nothing; here's all of me."* Something happened in those moments, in that dark living room. The best way I can explain it would be to say that it seemed like something, in some way, broke in me and over me. Whether in the heavens, or in my heart, or both, I don't know, but I had a strong sense that something significant had changed.

That was the moment of my surrender, my own Gethsemane, a "climax" in my Christian walk. Its "falling action" has never ceased to amaze me. God's Gethsemane crushed everything—my dreams, my music, my band, my relationships, my burgeoning opportunities; I should have been a mess, but I was the happiest I'd ever been, overflowing with an indescribable peace and true joy. I knew I was in God's will and my life was fully in his hands.

1. Is there any area in your life now that is causing spiritual anxiety, causing you to wrestle with God's will? Explain. What do you imagine your life will look like if you surrender to God's will on this?

_____

_____

_____

_____

_____

_____

_____

_____

_____

_____

2. Have you ever had a "Gethsemane" moment? If so, describe it. What was the "falling action?"

_____

_____

_____

_____

_____

_____

_____

_____

_____

_____

3. Do you believe that God has a general will for people's lives and holds us to a standard moral and ethical code? (Don't lie, cheat, steal, murder, fornicate, etc...) Describe the process by which a person discovers this code? If not, why not?

_____

_____

_____

_____

_____

_____

_____

_____

_____

_____

4. Do you believe that God has a specific will for your life? If not, why not? If so, how to you go about attempting to discover it and to live it out?

_____

_____

_____

_____

_____

_____

_____

_____

_____

_____

17

I'LL SHOW YOU WITH A KISS

Matthew 26:47-50

Judas, one of the twelve, with a great multitude with swords and clubs, came from the chief priests and elders of the people.

Now his betrayer had given them a sign, saying, "Whomever I kiss, he is the one; seize him." Immediately he went up to Jesus and said, "Greetings, Rabbi!" and kissed Him.

But Jesus said to him, "Friend, why have you come?"

Luke 22:47-48

And while he was still speaking, behold, a multitude; and he who was called Judas, one of the twelve, went before them and drew near to Jesus to kiss him. But Jesus said to him, "Judas, are you betraying the Son of Man with a kiss?"

WHO'S FOOLING WHO?

Let's think about this scene for a moment. Here comes Judas, creeping into the garden late at night with a gang of burly men, officers from the temple guard and an assortment of other rough and tumble dudes carrying swords, torches and clubs, snarling, looking mean, and ready for a fight... it looks like Jesus is about to get jumped! Then, in walks Judas, blithe and carefree, obviously oblivious to the roughneck gang behind him. He struts up to Jesus and greets him with a smile. Oh-so-happy is Judas to see his master. He acts as if he hasn't seen him in weeks. "Greetings, Rabbi!" he says glibly with outstretched arms. Embracing Jesus, he gives him a great big friendly kiss on the cheek. *Umm… who did this guy think he was fooling?* It appears, he was only fooling himself.

SELF-DECEPTION

The problem with deception is that it's deceiving… profound I know. James, the brother of Jesus, says, "Be doers of the Word, and not hearers only, *deceiving yourselves.*" (James 1:22) Self-deception is a real deal. Judas, the namesake of all betrayers, had to have himself deceived first in order to betray the Lord. He had to have himself convinced that what he was doing was for the best, at least for *his* best. He was a selfish pragmatist; the Apostle John just calls him a thief. A thief deals in deception and even the average thief is pragmatic; what they do almost always has a practical end. That practical end is their own good, their own gain. Someone who is self-deceived can be so convinced that what he or she is doing is for the best, that they can justify the worst and most horrible crimes. I am convinced that even Hitler, Stalin and Mao believed that, in the grand scheme of things, what they were doing was right. The human capacity for self-justification is almost limitless—self-deception at its best.

The self-deceived believes the lie, because he or she wants to believe the lie; it eases the conscience in the pursuit of the endgame—*their* desire, *their* happiness, *their* gain, or *their* pleasure. This endgame, this long or short term goal, fueled as it is by selfish motivation can lead to the betrayal of those we claim to love.

Betrayal means to deliver or expose someone to an enemy by treachery or disloyalty. When our sinful desires are at the forefront of our minds, when we are willing to act on them, disloyalty and treachery are never far behind. We are never truly free until we are free from having to please ourselves at other people's expense.

MOTIVES

While some motives are hidden, others can be quite obvious. I was flipping through the channels one night and caught an infomercial hosted by Reverend T. (I've cut the name to protect the guilty) There he was, white suit, perfectly slicked back hair, selling his little 40 page book, titled, (I wish I were making this up) *How to Get Rich and Have Everything You Ever Wanted!* Ok, here's a guy making a not-so-valiant effort to get some money and maybe a little fame. He uses the Lord and uses the name of the Lord to manipulate people, playing upon the human conscience and human greed to get what he wanted. His motives were, in general, much like Judas'.

Self-interest is necessary for survival, but can easily grow into something ugly and destructive. For Judas, self-interest turned into greed. For you, self-interest may turn into another one of the Top Forty favorites; lust, envy, jealousy, love of power, love of money, gluttony, revenge, anxiety, desire for control, desire for praise, etc. These things often drive manipulative and hypocritical action. The Bible says, "The heart is deceitful above all things, and desperately wicked; *Who can know it?* (Jeremiah 17:9) Who *can* know it? It seems obvious that Judas didn't.

THE KISS OF DEATH

So what's with the kiss? Other than a common greeting in Jesus' day, (though supposedly rare from student to master) it is the crescendo of Judas' hypocrisy. Even Jesus is like, "Seriously? A kiss? You betray me with a kiss?" A pointed finger would have been more honest. Perhaps, Judas wanted to keep from burning his bridges, hoping Jesus would save himself, reveal his true status and bring Judas with him in his ascension to power. Perhaps, he needed to protect himself from the other disciples, who might harm him for his betrayal? Perhaps, it was the ultimate self-deception, still keeping up appearances, convincing himself that, in the end, it would all turn out for the best.

After Judas kissed the Lord, Jesus asks him this interesting question, "Friend, *why* have you come?" In essence, "Friend, what's the real reason that you've come to me?" Judas doesn't answer this question, but it appears that the words of the Lord brought conviction of his betrayal; but what if he answered this question. If he were truthful, he would've had to say something to the effect of,

"To get what I want." We'd do well to ask ourselves this question from Jesus also. *Why do we come to the Lord?* What are the true motivations behind our actions? Why do we pray, worship, attend church, or read the Bible? In both our relationship with God and with others, it is important for us to examine ourselves. It is a betrayal to satisfy ourselves at other people's expense, especially at God's expense, even if we've convinced ourselves that it's all for the best.

Judas gives us an example of what not to do. Here, in the garden, we see why God commands us to not take the Lord's name in vain (Exodus 20:7). By his actions, Judas embodied a fuller meaning for this commandment. Judas was Jesus' disciple, and he took Jesus' name as his master, his Lord, but in the end, was it not in vain? With this in mind, with this human propensity for vainglory, it is best that we check our own motives. Is there any vanity, any selfish, self-seeking reasons why we take his name, why we go to church, or why we call ourselves Christian, why we minister, pray, preach, worship, etc.? Let's repent if necessary, lest our egocentric motives become for us our own kiss of death.

LIFE APPLICATIONS:

1. Are you in the habit of examining your own motives? Do you question yourself about why you do the things you do? If so, give some examples. What steps can you take to become more self-aware?

_____

_____

_____

_____

_____

_____

_____

_____

_____

2. Do you find it easy to soothe your own conscience by convincing yourself that your motives are pure? Can you think of a time in the past when you acted in "good conscience" but in retrospect realize that your motives behind those actions were less than pure. Give some examples of your own tendency for self-justification.

_____

_____

_____

_____

_____

_____

_____

_____

3.   Do you ever find yourself using religious expressions to accomplish a selfish goal? What examples have you seen of outward religious affection or actions that mask a selfishly motivated intent?

_____

_____

_____

_____

_____

_____

_____

_____

_____

4.   What would you describe as the primary motivations in life? Can you describe some situations in which these motivations either drove or drive you to manipulative and hypocritical action, or even betrayal? What steps can you take to change this behavior?

_____

_____

_____

_____

_____

_____

_____

_____

_____

18

THE ARREST

John 18:4-12

Jesus therefore, knowing all things that would come upon him, went forward and said to them, "Whom are you seeking?"

They answered him, "Jesus of Nazareth."

Jesus said to them, "I am he." And Judas, who betrayed him, also stood with them.

Now when he said to them, "I am he," they drew back and fell to the ground. Then, he asked them again, "Whom are you seeking?"

And they said, "Jesus of Nazareth."

Jesus answered, "I have told you that I am he. Therefore, if you seek me, let these go their way," that the saying might be fulfilled which he spoke, "Of those whom you gave me, I have lost none."

Then, Simon Peter, having a sword, drew it and struck the high priest's servant, and cut off his right ear.

But Jesus said to him, "Shall I not drink the cup which my Father has given me? Put your sword in its place, for all who take the sword will perish by the sword. Or do you think that I cannot now pray to my Father, and he will provide me with more than twelve legions of angels? How then could the Scriptures be fulfilled, that it must happen thus?"

In that hour, Jesus said to the multitudes, "Have you come out, as against a robber, with swords and clubs to take me? I sat daily with you, teaching in the temple, and you did not seize me. But all this was done that the Scriptures of the prophets might be fulfilled." Then, all the disciples forsook him and fled.

Then, the detachment of troops and the captain and the officers of the Jews arrested Jesus and bound him. And they led him away.

Mark 14:53-65

And they led Jesus away to the high priest; and with him were assembled all of the chief priests, the elders, and the scribes.

But Peter followed him at a distance, right into the courtyard of the high priest. And he sat with the servants and warmed himself at the fire.

Now the chief priests and all the council sought testimony against Jesus to put him to death, but found none. For many bore false witness against him, but their testimonies did not agree.

Then, some rose up and bore false witness against him, saying, "We heard him say, 'I will destroy this temple made with hands, and within three days I will build another made without hands.'" But not even then did their testimony agree.

And the high priest stood up in the midst and asked Jesus, saying, "Do you answer nothing? What *is it* these men testify against you?" But he kept silent and answered nothing.

Then, the high priest stood up and said to Jesus, "Are you not going to answer? What is this testimony that these men are bringing against you?" But Jesus remained silent.

The high priest said to him, "I charge you under oath by the living God: Tell us if you are the Christ, the Son of God."

"It is as you say, I am," Jesus replied. "Nevertheless, I say to you, hereafter you will see the Son of Man sitting at the right hand of Power, and coming on the clouds of heaven."

Then, the high priest tore his clothes and said, "He has spoken blasphemy! Why do we need any more witnesses? Look, now you have heard the blasphemy. What do you think?"

"He is worthy of death," they answered.

I AM HE

Jesus Christ, Son of God, willingly allows himself to be handed over, arrested, tried and convicted of crimes he didn't commit. We ought to take a moment to realize the enormity of this event. In this part of the SAVIOR Musical, we added an angelic chorus, watching in awe at this astounding moment in time. The love of God expressing itself in Jesus, God's son, the Christ, laying down his life for his creation. We have them sing in Hebrew- "*Barukh atah Adonai Eloheinu melekh ha'olam.*" It is translated: "Blessed are you, Lord, our God, king of the universe."

In this song, we attempt to focus attention on Jesus' repetition of, "I am he," at two key points of his arrest and trial. At each point, this declaration manifests and unveils Jesus' true nature. He is not merely a prophet, not just a wise man, not only a religious reformer; he is God come in human form. These two revelations force all who witness to make a personal judgment concerning Jesus of Nazareth.

So much is revealed during this arrest, but one moment jumps off the page to me. When Jesus asks the arrest mob who they're looking for; they reply, "Jesus of Nazareth." When he simply says, "I am he," the mob hits the ground… as if thrown down! This response, falling like dead men, is a common reaction in Scripture to encounters with God's glory (Daniel 8:18; Revelation 1:17), but I find it hard to get my head around this. *What just happened?* It's like the power of that statement from Jesus' mouth cracked open the window to his glory just a hair, only for a split second. Now, if I were of one these lackeys holding a weapon, trying to look tough with the rest of my mobster friends and three little words from our suspect knocks us all flat, I might rethink my plans, *Umm, do I really want to be a part of this?*

WILLING SACRIFICE

When these thugs get to their feet again, Peter decides to man up and take on the lot of them by himself and in the process, cuts off the ear of the High Priest's servant with a sword. Jesus, ever the teacher and ever looking out outside of himself, even when his own life is threatened, seizes the opportunity to teach a spiritual lesson. He doesn't need Peter's sword. Jesus demonstrates his faith and instructs us that trusting solely in own might and strength (by the sword) to save us, would be our downfall. Then the gospel of Luke tells us that Jesus healed the servant's ear. Again, if I'm of the garden variety arrest team and saw this, I may be reconsidering my options. Jesus reveals much about his nature and purpose as he instructs Peter that though he could easily prevent his own arrest by calling upon more than 12 legions of angels to aid him, he intends no such thing. Before we fly over that statement, let's do the math.

A legion ranged from 3,000-6,000 soldiers. So, if Jesus called more than twelve legions of angels, that could represent more than 72,000 heavenly warriors. That's a whole-lot-a angels! I think one angel would have sufficed. The point is clear. Whatever Peter imagines that it means for Jesus to be Messiah, Jesus reveals in signs Peter cannot ignore, that he intends to surrender to the Father's will, knowing full well what this entails. It was prophesied of old. From *this* Jesus, all the disciples, including Peter, scatter.

JESUS STANDS TRIAL

Jesus' next great "I am" announcement occurs at the end of his rather shady trial for various illegitimate charges. Here, in the dark hours, a league of leaders assembled, bent on Jesus' destruction. They gather phony witnesses to bring false accusation. Perhaps, if they paid more money, they could've gotten better liars, but as it is, they fail to carry the charges. If Jesus doesn't do something quick, they'll never convict him. Jesus uses a direct question from the High Priest to push the matter forward, making one of his most powerful statements concerning his true identity.

Caiaphas asks point blank, "Tell us if you are the Christ, the Son of God." Now, we must understand that the phrase "Son of God," was another term for messiah." The coming son of David, like all enthroned sons of David, were considered "the Son of God." (Psalm 2:7) So, Caiaphas asks in two forms, whether Jesus is the long awaited

Messiah. Jesus' answer is plain. He says, "I am."

Then, Jesus takes the matter further, revealing more about himself than was required. He responds prophetically, "Nevertheless, I say to you, hereafter you will see the Son of Man sitting at the right hand of power, and coming on the clouds of heaven." This is a profound revelation of Jesus' true identity in terms of the divine figure riding upon the clouds of heaven in Daniel 7:13, who receives all the power of the Kingdom of God from the Ancient of Days. He could have done little more to proclaim his own divine status before them. Disbelieving him, they seize upon his declaration as proof of blasphemy. He is tried and found guilty.

WHAT DO YOU THINK?

Blasphemy! Jesus' claims of being a divine messiah are not examined against fulfilled prophesy, miraculous healing, resurrection of the dead, power over demons, or other manifestations of divine power; they are automatically assumed to be blasphemy, an affront to divine glory. The High Priest asks, "What do you think?" They give their verdict, predetermined before the trial began, "He is worthy of death."

Preconceived notions, judgments without thought or investigation and the elevation of one's own reason above Scripture are dangerous standards for discerning the things of God.

The disciples had preconceived notions about who Jesus was and when those delusions were shattered, they scattered from him. It is the soul's habit to cast Jesus into many molds, to make him attractive to our own self-interests, to give him a cultural make-over in order to ease our own sensibilities, or lure the disinterested.

Jesus is still on trial today. He stands trial in every human heart that hears his gospel. We can become like these accusers when we cast our own shadows over Scripture, remaking Jesus in our own image. In this way, we put the real Jesus on the stand and declare, "He is worthy of death." So… *what do you think?* What's your verdict? Who is this Jesus to you… not in some religious sounding platitudes, but in truth?

LIFE APPLICATIONS:

1. What provokes you the most about the Jesus of Scripture? What aspects of the stories of Jesus do you find hardest to believe?

_____

_____

_____

_____

_____

_____

_____

_____

_____

_____

2. Can you list some things about the common Christian presentations of Jesus that you think are false? Can you give some examples from Scripture that make you think so?

_____

_____

_____

_____

_____

_____

_____

_____

_____

_____

3. Can you list some things about the common media presentations of Jesus (movies, TV, talk shows, news, etc.) that you think are false? What makes you think they are false presentations?

_____

_____

_____

_____

_____

_____

_____

_____

_____

_____

4. If you were sitting in that courtroom, heard his "I am" declarations, and the question was asked of you, "What do you think?" What would you say? What would be the basis for your answer?

_____

_____

_____

_____

_____

_____

_____

_____

_____

_____

19

PETER'S DENIAL

Matthew 26:58; 69-75

"Peter followed him at a distance to the high priest's courtyard. And he went in and sat with the servants to see the end. Now Peter sat outside in the courtyard. And a servant girl came to him, saying, "You also were with Jesus of Galilee."

But he denied it before them all, saying, "I do not know what you are saying."

And when he had gone out to the gateway, another girl saw him and said to those who were there, "This fellow also was with Jesus of Nazareth."

But again he denied with an oath, "I do not know the man!"

And a little later those who stood by came up and said to Peter, "Surely you also are one of them, for your speech betrays you."

Then, he began to curse and swear, saying, "I do not know the man!"

Immediately a rooster crowed. And Peter remembered the word of Jesus who had said to him, "Before the rooster crows, you will deny me three times." So he went out and wept bitterly.

BATTLE OF THE BANDS

Only a few months after the four of us had become Christians, our record label entered our band, The Trees, into a Battle of the Bands competition. Our drummer, Brian, informed us a few weeks before the competition, that he was praying, asking the Lord how our group could win... hoping, of course, God didn't like one of the other bands better. With great conviction, he said that the Lord told him we should play the only Christian song I'd written to that point. The song wasn't great. It was a slow, finger-picked ballad with only a *slightly Christian* meaning. Not the kind of song you'd play at a club, especially if you're trying to win a competition. Wanting, to be obedient to the Lord, however, we all committed to play that *Slightly Christian Song.*

The Campus Club in downtown Providence, Rhode Island was packed the night of the Battle of the Bands. Our whole following of friends and family came out to see us compete. The buzz in the place was electric, but shortly after our arrival at the club, Brian came up to me and said, "Hey man, Rich doesn't want to do that song."

"What do you mean?" I asked.

"Yeah, he says we should do..." I blanked out. *How could he do this, we are minutes from going on!* I decided to go calm down before speaking with Rich. I brought Dave up to speed. We were in agreement, but it was a conundrum. To ditch the *Slightly Christian Song* felt like ditching the Lord. Even if Brian's prophetic abilities were a tad skewed—do a Christian song, win the competition—our hearts told us we made a commitment to God we needed to keep.

I finally had a brief discussion with Rich. We had a good talk, "It's fine," he said. "Let's do the song." He shook my hand as the owner of our label, Big Noise Records, took the stage and began introducing some of the biggest record labels, publications and promoters from New York... his special guests:

"I'd like to introduce *so and so* from RCA records, and *this guy* from Rolling Stone magazine and *whose-a-fish* from Sony records." I remember this next part like it was yesterday—there's Rich, absently still shaking my hand with his head turned around watching all these big-wig music execs stand up from their round tables to receive their introduction. With the words 'It's fine, let's do the song,' still lingering in the air, he turns back to me with horror on his face, shaking his head, saying, "We can't do that song!"

I didn't know what to do. I was stunned. I said something like, "I can't talk about this right now," and walked away to gather myself. I explained the situation to Dave, then Brian approached us with a mangled expression and said, "We can't do that song." Fearing we were being pulled apart, wishing, at that moment, that I'd never even written it. I said to Dave, "Let's just forget it; it's just a stupid song!" I was freaking out inside, but Dave's typical calm demeanor helped hold me together.

As our time slot grew closer, this truly turned into a battle of the bands. At issue, as we discovered through talking together and the ensuing meltdown, was a general embarrassment and fear on Brian and Rich's part. They didn't want to stand up in front of those musical Big Wigs, and their mocking and needling friends and sing about their commitment to Christ. This was their big chance and they didn't want to blow it. As the tensions mounted, Brian started drinking and smoking... two habits he'd recently given up. At one point, our band and many of our supporters ended up outside the club arguing. Some of Rich and Brian's friends were giving them a hard time, saying, "Come on! You're not going to play a Christian song are you?" So, Brian and Rich gave us an ultimatum: they weren't going to play *at all* if it meant playing that song. They weren't ready to take that kind of a stand for Christ and truthfully, it was tough for me too. I thank God for Dave's faith and for sending a strong Christian couple from our church, who picked up on what was happening, gave us wise council and prayed with us. It encouraged me.

Dave and I stuck it out, and with three minutes to go before we were on, the guys begrudgingly agreed to play the *Slightly Christian Song*. Now a finger-picked, acoustic song in a loud nightclub usually doesn't go over well, but as we started playing, a hush came over the place. Everyone stopped and listened. When we finished, the judges panel in front of us held up their scorecards—all tens. We won!

Then, we broke up.

THE DENIAL

I think the Apostle Peter would understand Brian's and Rich's struggle. Imagine this; Peter, who, only moments before, waded into a mob of armed guards with a sword to defend Jesus, now cowers before a servant girl, denying the very Lord he claimed he would die for. What happened? I'm not a behavioral psychologist, but it seems that his belief system collapsed. Saying, "I'd die for you," when you think you won't is a different matter than even associating yourself with a condemned man. His denial springs from fear, a profound instinct for self-preservation. He follows at a distance; he tries to blend in with the crowd, vows no knowledge of Jesus, takes up cursing, puts on Groucho glasses... Indeed, before the cock crows twice, he denies Jesus thrice. (Try saying that 5 times fast.)

Peter's actions portray a digression in his choices from his shocked disappointment at Jesus' arrest to his terrified cursing, and overt denial. The night of the Battle of the Bands was, for our group, the battle of our souls... would we, or wouldn't we, stand publicly for Jesus, no matter what it cost us? We all wage this battle at one time or another, in one way or another. Denial at one point is not total failure, as Peter will show, but it is part of a dangerous slide toward an ultimate betrayal of Christ, as Judas will show. That profound desire to fit in with the crowd, to find safety, security and acceptance can easily lead to a digression of our choices, an embrace of this world and all its corruption and a forsaking of our faith in the Lord.

While life remains, hope remains. Peter's confrontation of his own cowardice, his own capacity for weakness, revealed in the foretold crowing, drives him to bitter weeping. Jesus, whose rejection of messianic glory in favor of arrest and humiliation rattled Peter's faith in him, now rises anew in Peter's heart as the true prophet; he foretold this very denial, and expressed love, understanding and forgiveness in the prediction of it. He said, "Simon, Simon! Indeed, Satan has asked for you, that he may sift you as wheat. But I have prayed for you, that your faith should not fail; and when you have returned to me, strengthen your brethren." (Luke 22:31-32)

This prayer shows the heart of God for all who have denied him in any form or fashion. We've all denied Christ in some way. There is beauty in understanding our own weakness, but only when reflected upon through his strength. Again, while life remains, while time remains, hope remains. We can, like Peter, turn and embrace Jesus' prayer—that our *faith not fail*, but we *return* to him and *live* to strengthen others.

LIFE APPLICATIONS:

1. Have you ever felt a powerful embarrassment, fear, or nervousness about being associated with Christ or his church? If so, share some of your experiences.

_____

_____

_____

_____

_____

_____

_____

_____

_____

_____

2. Have you ever specifically changed your behavior to fit in, doing things you knew were wrong to prevent association with Jesus, or his Church? If so, share some of your experiences.

_____

_____

_____

_____

_____

_____

_____

_____

_____

_____

3. Have you ever outright denied the Lord? If so, looking back can you see the process of disintegration in your behavior before it happened? If so, talk about it. Have you been restored, or do you need to respond like Peter and repent?

_____

_____

_____

_____

_____

_____

_____

_____

_____

_____

4. Have you ever come through an experience like Peter's that caused you to confront your own weakness, driving you to repentance, but leading you to become a stronger, more faithful person? Talk about it.

_____

_____

_____

_____

_____

_____

_____

_____

_____

20

TAKE IT BACK

Matthew 27:3-6

When Judas, who had betrayed him, saw that Jesus was condemned, he was seized with remorse and returned the thirty pieces of silver to the chief priests and the elders. "I have sinned," he said, "for I have betrayed innocent blood."

"What is that to us?" they replied. "That's your responsibility."

So Judas threw the money into the temple and left. Then he went away and hanged himself.

The chief priests picked up the coins and said, "It is against the law to put this into the treasury, since it is blood money." So they decided to use the money to buy the potter's field as a burial place for foreigners. That is why it has been called the Field of Blood to this day. Then what was spoken by Jeremiah the prophet was fulfilled: "They took the thirty pieces of silver, the price set on him by the people of Israel, and they used them to buy the potter's field, as the Lord commanded me." NIV

MY FRIEND

I met Troy in Bible college. Before attending, he had been delivered from a crack cocaine addiction in a Christian program, called *Teen Challenge*. Troy was a great guy—good-looking with a huge personality and a gregarious preaching style. My church fell in love with him, and we became fast friends.

Early one morning, I awoke to pounding at my door. I opened it to find Troy as I'd never seen him—disturbed, disheveled and fidgety. "What's up, Troy?" I asked, trying to wipe the sleep from my eyes.

"I have to talk to you," he said and motioned for me to follow him. Something was wrong. Troy led me to a beat up old car that I didn't recognize and got in the driver's seat. I got in next to him. His fingers were burnt black and shaking as he tried to smoke a tiny cigarette butt. Troy squirmed in his seat as he told me that he'd slipped up, that he'd been bingeing all night on crack. He began to cry, but when I tried to console him, he interrupted me, saying he needed money really bad. The beat-up car belonged to a drug dealer to whom he owed money.

Troy was living on campus, and, so, I told him we should go back, but this provoked him. I tried to give him other options, but he only grew more anxious and fidgety. He said he was worried for his life, and, looking at him, I realized that, in his state of desperation, he might do something drastic to get it, perhaps, hurt someone. It was breaking my heart. Not knowing what else to do, I gave him some money.

That night, my pastor called me. Troy's binge was over. He'd returned to school, and was sleeping peacefully. I was relieved he was safe. I didn't know it at the time, but I would never see Troy alive again. He was kicked out of school upon waking and returned to his hometown in Louisiana in shame, diving deeper and deeper into his old crack addiction. I was notified a short time later that Troy was dead. He left a suicide note saying that he couldn't go on letting God and everyone else down. He couldn't live under the weight of guilt and remorse anymore.

REPENTANCE vs. SELF-CONDEMNATION

Troy was not a "Judas," but both Troy and Judas fatally succumbed to that common plague—*self-condemnation.* Self-condemnation is a critical inward fixation on our failures. In the SAVIOR song, *Take It Back*, Judas laments, "You can take this pain, 'cause I can't carry this weight." Realizing what he has done, he returns the 30 silver coins and declares Jesus' innocence to the chief priests and elders. When these attempts to ease his guilty conscience fail, he hangs himself. Self-condemnation doesn't always result in suicide, but Judas and Troy couldn't break free from the weight of it and were mortally crushed.

We all fail in different ways and in varying degrees in life. The only thing we have left after we mess up, however, after we are convicted of sin, is our response. We can respond to conviction with repentance, embracing forgiveness and seeking change, or we can respond to conviction with self-condemnation, attempting to atone for our sins through self-inflicted punishment and penance. Self-atonement is our way of maintaining control, of taking matters into our own hands; it competes with Christ's atonement. True repentance leads the sinner to the SAVIOR.[iii]

Conviction is that God-given sense of wrongdoing meant to drive us back to God and his chosen path for our lives. Conviction works like a guardrail, letting us know when we're going off track. It hurts to hit a guardrail, but it is a good thing, if we allow it to do its intended work, saving us from greater harm and sending us back onto the road. Conviction is an inner reminder from God's Spirit, letting us know that we are not where we need to be. It seeks to protect us from us, and others from us, as our selfish behavior threatens both our present and eternal wellbeing.

Self-condemnation, however, has a different affect. Distraught over hitting the guardrail, self-condemnation drives us through the rail and over the cliff, thinking, *Serves me right.* Like Judas, there is a temptation when we sin to cast off all restraint, indulging further yet. It's the diet-breaker syndrome that says, "Well, forget it now!!! I blew it!!! MacDonald's® here I come!" In these moments, we'd do well to take a lesson from Peter when he failed the Lord—the Word of God and the Spirit of God has the power to bring the kind of conviction that causes us to repent, getting us back on track. After all, a living dog is better than a dead lion.

PETER AND JUDAS

How we respond to failure and sin is critical to our spiritual lives. In the events leading up to the arrest and conviction of Jesus, we see Peter and Judas. The greatest of the disciples and the worst of the disciples... yet, they both failed the Lord. We could distinguish the motives behind their actions, for while Peter, in a moment of weakness and panic, denied even knowing Jesus; Judas' actions were premeditated, plotting against and betraying Jesus, his master. Peter failed through *weakness*, and Judas through overt *wickedness*. There is a difference between *weakness* and *wickedness*, but the real difference between these two men was not their particular brand of sin, but their responses to their sins. Peter's response was of humility and repentance. He wept bitterly over his failures and his heart drew close to Christ once again. Judas, however full of remorse for his *betrayal*, sank under the weight of self-condemnation. His response was self-centered and, seeking escape from his anguish, *he went out and hung himself*.

Two men. Two failures. Two responses. Two paths: humility and repentance/pride and self-destruction. Peter, the denier, became the greatest of the disciples, and Judas... he became the namesake of all betrayers. It is God's purpose to redeem us, and he uses conviction to get our attention.

In moments of deep remorse and self-condemnation, as consumed as we are with the guilt of what we've done and the consequences of our actions, we must remember that there is no sin too great for Christ's forgiveness. It is at these moments of conviction that our belief in the goodness and mercy of God is most required, our dependency on his Spirit and strength most necessary, our repentance most vital. Our responses to conviction take us either farther away from the God who loves us, or closer to him.

LIFE APPLICATIONS:

1. In your own terms, describe conviction, repentance & self-condemnation.

_____

_____

_____

_____

_____

_____

_____

_____

_____

_____

2. Contrast times in your life when you responded to a conviction of personal sin with self-condemnation versus repentance.

_____

_____

_____

_____

_____

_____

_____

_____

_____

_____

3. Tell about a time when you attempted to self-atone, to remedy a sinful situation on your own without God, confession and/or repentance.

_____

_____

_____

_____

_____

_____

_____

_____

_____

_____

4. Like the diet-breaker, do you find yourself casting off restraint once you've fallen into a sin? Is confession and repentance, grace and forgiveness sufficient to ease your conscience and help you break these habits? Explain.

_____

_____

_____

_____

_____

_____

_____

_____

_____

_____

5. Are there sins from your past that still provoke self-condemnation? Would confession and repentance, grace and forgiveness be sufficient to ease your conscience? Why? Are there people, against whom you've sinned, to whom you need to make confession and seek forgiveness? If so, how do you think you should do it?

_____

_____

_____

_____

_____

_____

_____

_____

_____

_____

6. What would you say to someone contemplating suicide, who is buried under the weight of deep remorse and self-condemnation?

_____

_____

_____

_____

_____

_____

_____

_____

21

A LAMB TO THE SLAUGHTER

Matthew 26:67-68

Then, they spit in his face and struck him with their fists. Others slapped him and said, "Prophesy to us, Christ. Who hit you?" NIV

Matthew 27:1-2

When morning came, all the chief priests and elders of the people plotted against Jesus to put him to death. And when they had bound him, they led him away and delivered him to the governor, Pontius Pilate.

ANGRY CHRISTIAN

Early in my Christian walk, shortly after I'd finished writing the SAVIOR Musical, what we were then calling "The King of All Kings," we held a few performances with a full band at my church. What was most miraculous to me was that, while I started this project knowing no musicians in my new Christian community, other than Dave, of course, God seemed to draw them out of the woodwork to create not only a solid stage production, but also a decent multi-track recording. It was an exciting time for everyone... well, almost everyone. One person wasn't so amazed. We'll call him Angry Christian... as good a John Bunyan character as you ever hoped to meet.

The offerings from these performances allowed us to purchase a new sound system for the church. I was at the church late one night, listening to part of the recording on the church's new speakers when the whole system blew. The next day, my friend, John, and I tried to get the speakers to work, but they were fried. The service was fast approaching, and Angry Christian, the worship leader that night, who resented the liberty the pastor granted me in the church, finally showed up. When told the system was shot, he lost it. He totally freaked out. He started screaming at me right there in the sanctuary.

Now, in the days of bygone, I wouldn't have tolerated anyone speaking to me this way, even if I were wrong... never mind that I hadn't done anything inappropriate with the system... never mind that my ministry purchased the stupid things. On that day, however, I had a bizarre calm. I didn't need to defend myself. I merely squeaked out, "I'm sorry." My friend John had me go next door to fellowship hall while he tried to calm down Angry Christian.

When the pastor arrived, I became nervous. *He's going to kill me,* I thought. I could hear yelling next door and when my pastor came into the fellowship hall, he just said to me, "Listen, we're in the people business, not the speaker business." That was a powerful lesson for me. My pastor showed grace and put the situation into it's proper perspective. He took a different approach with Angry Christian, however, when we all discovered that the speakers blew because Angry Christian had wired them wrong.

MISTREATMENT

If you're reading this and living in the same fallen and broken world that I am, then, chances are, you have been mistreated at some point in your life. Either at work, at home, at school, even at church, we are constantly afforded opportunities to respond to mistreatment.

We're all inclined to feel that we are being mistreated when caught and punished for our wrongdoings, or poor performance, but that's *not* what we're talking about here. The kind of mistreatment we're discussing occurs when we suffer abuse, in one form or another, unjustly, unfairly, randomly, or even specifically for doing good.

Jesus was abandoned, arrested, rejected, humiliated, falsely accused, wrongfully charged, beaten and taunted... and for what? He went about doing good: feeding the hungry, healing the sick, preaching good news to the poor, teaching about the kingdom of God; he lived a life of love and charity. So, why didn't he stand up for himself during this trial? He had the authority and every right to cry, "Foul." Yet, he doesn't defend himself, complain of the injustice, or fight back. Instead, he is silent. The prophet, Isaiah, predicted that he would be. "He was oppressed and he was afflicted, yet he opened not his mouth; he was led as *a lamb to the slaughter*, and as a sheep before its shearers is silent, so he opened not his mouth." (Isaiah 53:7)

HIS RESPONSE

The Apostle Peter, having come through his own personal trial, has this to say about it:

> "What credit is it if, when you are beaten for your faults, you take it patiently? But when you do good and suffer, if you take it patiently, this *is* commendable before God. For *to this you were called*, because Christ also suffered for us, leaving us an *example*, that you should *follow his steps:* 'Who committed no sin, Nor was deceit found in his mouth;' who, when he was reviled, did not revile in return; when he suffered, he did not threaten, but committed *himself* to him who judges righteously." (1 Peter 2:20-23)

"To *this* you were called," Peter says. Called to what? Called to use Christ's *example, following* in *his steps* when responding to unjust treatment. Jesus didn't lie to get out of trouble. He didn't fall to cursing and reviling those attacking him. He didn't resort to threats of reprisal. Instead, he cast himself into the hands of God, who sees all, judges right and has a plan.

HIS PURPOSE

Jesus responded in many ways over the years of his ministry to various threats and confrontations. In every situation, including his silent embrace of suffering at the hands of wicked men after his arrest, his singular goal was to advance God's kingdom among men. Christ suffered with a purpose. "…Jesus, the author and finisher of our faith, who, *for the joy that was set before him*, endured the cross, despising the shame..." (Hebrews 12:1-2) "For Christ also suffered once for sins, the just for the unjust, *that he might bring us to God*." (1 Peter 3:18a)

Jesus did not react out of a desire to defend his reputation, or to accomplish some selfish goal, or to alleviate his discomfort. Christ's purpose in allowing himself to endure unjust treatment from which he might have easily escaped, was to fulfill the will of the Father in bringing us to God. Jesus did not see those driving him to the cross as obstacles to his purpose; they *were* his purpose.

OUR RESPONSE vs. HIS PURPOSE

So how do you typically handle mistreatment? Are you just like Jesus when your delightful day is ruined by encountering the selfish idiocy of some clod? When mistreatment comes our way, we can lose our religion fast and furious. It's easy to get so caught up in *our* purposes that we forget about God's. In moments of mistreatment, we easily forget that God uses suffering to *train* us, to perform a work in and through us. "Now no chastening seems to be joyful for the present, but painful; nevertheless, afterward it yields the peaceable fruit of righteousness to those who have been *trained* by it." (Hebrews 12:11)

We can read this Scripture and think, *Yes, we are being trained, that's so true*, but get in our cars and merge into rush hour traffic… the moment that guy cuts us off, it's "Training? What training? I'm gonna train him!" Ok, so dealing with rush hour traffic isn't exactly suffering for Jesus, but it illustrates the point; somehow, we've got it in our minds that we must look out for number one, must be respected, must preserve our reputations. When we fuss and fume and struggle to have things our way, however, we lose his way. We come to see other people as obstacles to our purposes, rather than actually BEING OUR PURPOSES.

We are born with an inner sense of fairness. "That's not fair,"

seems to be some of the first words out of the mouths of babes...
right after, "Mine!!!" When we realize, however, that God uses
mistreatment at the hands of others to strengthen our trust in him,
who judges righteously, it builds patience and self-control. In those
many moments of being treated unfairly in this broken and unfair
world, think of your training. Think of Christ willingly enduring
unimaginable suffering at the hands of wicked men to open a path to
God for sinners just like them... just like you. We can conclude with
no better admonition than Peter's Words in 1 Peter 3:8-17.

> "Finally, all of you, have unity of mind, sympathy,
> brotherly love, a tender heart, and a humble mind. Do
> not repay evil for evil or reviling for reviling, but on
> the contrary, bless, for to this you were called, that
> you may obtain a blessing. For whoever desires to
> love life and see good days, let him keep his tongue
> from evil and his lips from speaking deceit; let him
> turn away from evil and do good; let him seek peace
> and pursue it. For the eyes of the Lord are on the
> righteous, and his ears are open to their prayer. But
> the face of the Lord is against those who do evil.
> Now who is there to harm you if you are zealous for
> what is good? But even if you should suffer for
> righteousness' sake, you will be blessed. Have no fear
> of them, nor be troubled, but in your hearts honor
> Christ the Lord as holy, always being prepared to
> make a defense to anyone who asks you for a reason
> for the hope that is in you; yet do it with gentleness
> and respect, having a good conscience, so that, when
> you are slandered, those who revile your good
> behavior in Christ may be put to shame. For it is
> better to suffer for doing good, if that should be
> God's will, than for doing evil." (ESV)

LIFE APPLICATIONS:

1. Name some areas in your life where God may have used, or may be using mistreatment to do a work in you (training) and through you (mission). For instance, lack of respect, mockery, people talking behind your back, etc. Share some specific instances.

_____

_____

_____

_____

_____

_____

_____

_____

_____

_____

_____

2. Briefly describe what you believe God's purpose for your life to be. Does this help you to deal well with unjust treatment? Explain.

_____

_____

_____

_____

_____

_____

_____

_____

_____

_____

3. Do you strive harder "to be right," than to "be used" to do a good work in the lives of those who mistreat you? Do you tend to think of yourself as an example, as a representative of Jesus Christ, as you go about your day? Explain.

_____

_____

_____

_____

_____

_____

_____

_____

_____

_____

4. Do you struggle with un-forgiveness, vengefulness and/or defensiveness when you feel mistreated? What are some ways you can diffuse your own defensive nature, anger and pride during times of trial and unjust treatment?

_____

_____

_____

_____

_____

_____

_____

_____

22

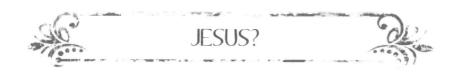

JESUS?

John 18:28-32

They led Jesus from Caiaphas to the Praetorium, and it was early morning. But they themselves did not go into the Praetorium, lest they should be defiled, but that they might eat the Passover. Pilate then went out to them and said, "What accusation do you bring against this man?"

They answered and said to him, "If he were not an evildoer, we would not have delivered him up to you."

Then, Pilate said to them, "You take him and judge him according to your law."

Therefore, the Jews said to him, "It is not lawful for us to put anyone to death," that the saying of Jesus might be fulfilled which he spoke, signifying by what death he would die.

Luke 23:2

And they began to accuse him, saying, "We found this man perverting the nation, and forbidding to pay taxes to Caesar, saying that he himself is Christ, a king."

CONTACT

Ever see the movie *Contact*? I'll pretend you haven't. In the movie, a scientist receives a message from outer space. It's just a pulse of sound waves… or is it? [Spoiler Alert!] They discover that the sound waves have layers of data attached to it. Soon scientists from all around the world are scrambling to decode this alien data file. When they finally do, they realize what it is—a set of instructions on how to build a space module that will take one earthling through a wormhole to… well, I won't give any more of it away, but it's a great movie.

Sometimes I think I received a similar alien package that has taken me years to decode. Shortly after I quit my band, I had a morning wakeup call with a package delivery from deep in outer space. It was a little tune pulsing in my head. I went downstairs to an old hand-me-down organ I had in my living room and started plunking it out. Then, I realized lyrics were attached to it…

"Jesus? Who is this man they call Jesus?

Who is this man he should teach us?

Why have they sent him to me…"

Oh, I thought, *I know who this is… it's Pilate… wait… I know what this is!* The package, it turned out, was filled with song after song; it downloaded for a month straight—a month of music, real God-given music like I'd never known. It was incredible; I loved it! Words and melodies flowed naturally as if the Holy Spirit was downloading songs for me to write. I didn't know how it all would turn out, I was just writing… though it felt more like decoding, and at the end of 30 days, the SAVIOR Musical was born. I'd like to say that angels and shepherds were in attendance, but mostly it was me and my dog, Franny.

WHY HAVE THEY SENT HIM TO ME?

In writing this piece, this first of many songs, I got to thinking about Pontius Pilate. At the time of Christ, Israel was occupied by Rome. He was the Roman governor appointed over Judea and had come to Jerusalem for the Passover feast. I thought about what it must have been like for him. Here is a Roman, who could care less about the Jewish religion, being pressed to make a difficult decision in regards to their Messiah.

Jesus has been condemned by the Jewish council, declared worthy of death. Unfortunately, they don't have the power to carry out the sentence under Roman law. They want Pilate to execute him for them... and not in a blind alley either. It must be public; it must be official. His accusers lead Jesus to the Praetorium, (i.e. the governor's palace) where Roman justice was administered.

The song, "Jesus," the first of the Pilate pieces, contains imaginings of Pilate's thoughts. They illustrate the difficulty Pilate likely has making a decision about the identity of this man.

DECISIONS

Pilate had some tough decisions to make. The coming chapters will unpack some of these, but the first decision concerns the question of identity—*Who is this man they call Jesus?* This is the question of the ages, and it presents itself to every soul hearing the gospel. Pilate certainly didn't want to have to answer this question; in fact, he's rather annoyed at being drawn into Jewish religious affairs. Like Pilate, many today don't want to have to answer this question either, but hearing the audacity and enormity of Jesus' claims demands an answer. If he is who he says he is, then someday, whether on this or that side of the grave, every knee shall bow and every tongue shall confess that Jesus is Lord. If he is not who he claims to be, then Jesus is the greatest fraud in human history and his Church is a lie.

WHO DO YOU SAY THAT I AM?

The identity of Jesus is a recurring theme in the gospels. Jesus makes many claims about himself, and performs many works to manifest himself, and the gospels record the various conclusions that people make concerning his identity. Even unclean spirits get in on the act, having, it seems, the clearest picture of who he is. They shout out things like, "I know who you are—the Holy One of God!" (Mark 1:24) or, "What have I to do with you Jesus, son of the most high

God!" (Mark 5:7) People, however, have a harder time with this one.

When Jesus asks his disciples, "Who do men say that I am?" They reply, 'Some say John the Baptist, some Elijah, and others Jeremiah or one of the prophets.' We might expand on this as we read other responses. The people call him teacher, Rabbi, master, lord (with a small el). Some of his relatives call him a madman. The religious leaders say he is a demon-possessed fraud, a blasphemer, a drunk, a deceiver of the people.

When, however, he asks his disciples directly, "Who do *you* say that I am?" Simon Peter answered, "You are the Christ, the Son of the living God." Pleased, Jesus replies, "Blessed are you, Simon Bar-Jonah, for flesh and blood has not revealed *this* to you, but my Father who is in heaven." (Matthew 16:13-17)

After everything they saw him do and everything they heard him say, Jesus still regards the heart's discovery of his true identity as a point of divine revelation. Understanding the identity of Christ is not purely a cognitive matter, or a matter of mere deduction; it is also a spiritual matter. It is contact from heaven, a message from God downloaded into the human heart—Jesus is God, worthy of all praise and endless devotion.

One of two things confronts us here.

Those who have come into the church, who love the community, who enjoy the music, who find comfort in the preaching of good living and stable home, still need a revelation of the identity of Jesus not just in the mind, but in the heart. We all need a revelation from the Father about his son. We all need to pray, and seek it from him.

Those who have had this contact, whose hearts have already been opened to the truth of Jesus Christ, must remember what salvation really is—a confrontation of the heart with Jesus Christ that results in repentance and devotion and comes, ultimately, only through a revelation from God. While we should reason about Jesus, we cannot reason people to Jesus. While we should defend our faith, we cannot argue people into salvation. While we should love people, and while Jesus declared our love a powerful witness for him, it is only when hearts make contact with the Holy, receiving revelation from God of who Jesus truly is that people enter into his "kingdom."

Remember Paul's proof of true discipleship, "For we know, brothers loved by God, that he has chosen you, because our gospel came to you not only in word, but also in power and in the Holy Spirit and with full conviction." (I Thessalonians 1:4-5)

LIFE APPLICATIONS:

1. Describe who you believe Jesus is. How did you come to this conclusion? Was there a moment in time when you had your own contact experience, a time when you came to this realization? If so, describe it.

_____

_____

_____

_____

_____

_____

_____

_____

_____

_____

2. If you were honest with yourself, would you say that you have been committed to Jesus Christ, or have you been mainly committed to Christianity, and/or church, or to none of these? Explain. Are you in a place now where you feel you need a new revelation of Jesus Christ?

_____

_____

_____

_____

_____

_____

_____

_____

_____

_____

3. If you are a disciple of Jesus Christ, would you honestly describe your evangelistic efforts in terms of introducing people to Jesus, or in terms of winning them to the Christian community? Describe the difference.

_____

_____

_____

_____

_____

_____

_____

_____

_____

_____

23

IS IT TRUE?

Matthew 27:11-14

Now Jesus stood before the governor. And the governor asked him, saying, "Are you the King of the Jews?"

Jesus said to him, "It is as you say." And while he was being accused by the chief priests and elders, he answered nothing.

Then, Pilate said to him, "Do you not hear how many things they testify against you?" But he answered him not one word, so that the governor *marveled greatly*.

"THE GOVERNOR MARVELED GREATLY"

Pontius Pilate was not a man who cared about the Jewish religion—he was a Roman, after all. The Roman culture valued honor, pride, dignity and strength far more than ethereal religion. They believed these attributes were only achieved through dominance, military might and iron fisted rule. It is no wonder that Pilate *marveled greatly* at Christ's response to his accusers. He'd seen many men in Christ's position—accused and facing death, groveling, defending themselves, and begging mercy, anything in an attempt to save their own hides. From Jesus, however, zip, zilch, zero, nada...

What Pilate was witnessing was so unbelievable that he wanted to check Jesus' hearing... "Do you not hear how many things they testify against you?" I suppose Pilate really wanted to yell out, "Hey, Dummy, theeeey waaaaaant tooooooo kiiiiiill yoooooooou! Defend yourself!!!" Christ, however, appealed to a higher power and a greater judge and didn't have to answer his accusers. This blew Pilate's mind.

A TRIAL

A few years ago, while living in a Nashville, Tennessee apartment complex, called The Summit, where my wife, Britney, worked, I sold my truck to a guy. A friend of his that had been at the sale came to pick up the title for him a few nights later. Once I went downstairs and handed it to him, he stepped up on the stoop, and blocked my path back into the apartment building. Then, he said, "Hold on. See, here's the thing. You don't know me, and... aahh... we're going to keep the truck, but... aahh... we want the money back." He was fidgety and nervous, ten years and, perhaps, fifty pounds my junior... definitely hyped up on something.

When I said, "I'm not going to give you the money back," he started looking around and fishing in his pockets. Having no intention of waiting for him to muster the courage to pull a weapon, I shove past him to walk back upstairs. That's when he maced me with pepper spray. Options suddenly appeared:

Option 1: Beat the tar out of him.
Option 2: Continue upstairs, turning my back on an attacker.
Option 3: Restrain him.

I chose option 3. I grabbed him and launched off the stoop, over a bush, crashing upside down onto the sidewalk. I landed heavily on top of him. My face was already beginning to burn, and my eyes were blurring from the mace.

I snatched him from the ground and tried to constrain him. Failing that, I tried to get the fight out of him by bouncing him off the cement a few times, ending up on top of him at the bottom of the stairwell. He was helpless, but took to pulling my hair to break free. In comes my wife, riding upon a white stallion. I looked up, bleary-eyed, as Britney rushed down the stairs, screaming, "Get your hands off of my husband!" She started clawing his hands, and he pleaded, "Get him off me!"

There I am, trying to calm her down, all the while fishing through his pockets for ID, or any weapons he might have. I handed her whatever I found and sent her upstairs to call the police. Someone from the parking lot suddenly screamed, "Hey, get off him!" *His friend!* I thought. Picking up my new battered companion from the stairs and holding him in a headlock and by the top of his underwear, I staggered into the parking lot to confront the voice. When he got close enough for my pepper sprayed eyes to make him out, I was relieved; it was the night security guard. *Oh, good,* I thought, but he was yelling at me to let the kid go, then I saw he had his hand on his pistol. *Oh not good...* he took me for the villain. I tried to tell him what was going on, but with his hand on his gun, I decided it best to let go. As soon as I did, the poor kid limped off, clothes shredded, holding an injured shoulder. The guard went after him. I went upstairs to put out the fire that was searing my face and eyes.

Eventually, we all ended up outside with Britney's boss, who ran the complex, listening to the security guard's tale of how the kid tried to evade him by jumping over a guard rail. "I approached him, asking him if he was alright," the security guard recalled. Then he told me to get away from him and ran toward the road, then leaped over the guardrail... he just vanished into thin air," he said. The place was called The Summit for a good reason. The other side of that rail was a 35 to 40 foot drop straight down into a grassy field. Somehow, the poor soul eventually managed to limp away.

PEOPLE WATCH YOU

People watch how you respond during trials. Struggles reveal us. As Christians, they can reveal our faith for good, or ill. It can be hard to keep this in mind when we're the ones going through the fire.

When the Security Guard was finished relaying his tale, we purveyed the scene of the crime and found a large knife that the kid had dropped. Even knowing this, that I could have been stabbed, or worse, I'm still not sure if I chose the right option or not. I didn't enjoy throwing him around. I couldn't help but feel bad for the kid. At the risk of sounding super-spiritual, I honestly thought, *What horrible wages Satan gives to his servants.* He was obviously lost and I wanted to help him, to tell him about our hope in Christ. The security guard thought he was on methamphetamines, which made me feel even worse for him. I kept saying, "I feel so bad for him."

Britney's boss shook his head, "I can't believe you feel bad for that kid," he said smiling; "He deserved getting hurt, he could have killed you!" He was impressed, but I wasn't trying to put on a compassion show—*Look at me, I'm soooo spiritual.* I was honestly upset that someone could fall so low (No pun intended).

A GOOD RESPONSE GOES A LONG WAY

As Britney's boss walked back to his place, I heard him tell the security guard, "He's a minister. I can't believe this, what a great guy." *Well, shucks…* I realized what a powerful, but unintended, impact it had on him. Britney told me that her boss talked for some time thereafter about the event and my reaction. For me, the lesson was clear, "Hey, I really *am* a great guy." Just kidding. I learned that if you call yourself a Christian, people look for Jesus in you… *especially* when you're tried.

Please know that I could've told you a number of stories of when I've blown it, but I see in this experience a small glimmer (really small) of what Pilate may have experienced. In times of trial, there can be great spiritual results in others who witness our Christ-like spirit. When we trust God with our lives and live for his purposes. When we regard others not as obstacles to our purpose, but *as* our purpose, it has a profound impact on those who witness it. Pilate saw this in Christ and he *marveled greatly.*

LIFE APPLICATIONS:

1. How has witnessing Christians' responses to conflict and trials impacted you? Do you have a sense of being a witness for Christ in the way that you respond to daily trials and conflicts? Explain.

_____

_____

_____

_____

_____

_____

_____

_____

_____

_____

2. Share an experience where you feel that you represented Christ well in a moment of trial.

_____

_____

_____

_____

_____

_____

_____

_____

_____

_____

3. Share an experience where you feel that you did *not,* represent Christ well in a moment of trial.

_____

_____

_____

_____

_____

_____

_____

_____

_____

_____

4. What do you think you could do to stay aware of your witness during a time of conflict or trial?

_____

_____

_____

_____

_____

_____

_____

_____

_____

_____

_____

24

THE KING OF THE JEWS

John 18:33-38

Then, Pilate entered the Praetorium again, called Jesus, and said to him, "Are you the King of the Jews?" Jesus answered him, "Are you speaking for yourself about this, or did others tell you this concerning me?"

Pilate answered, "Am I a Jew? Your own nation and the chief priests have delivered you to me. What have you done?"

Jesus answered, "My kingdom is not of this world. If my kingdom were of this world, my servants would fight, so that I should not be delivered to the Jews; but now my kingdom is not from here."

Pilate therefore said to him, "Are you a king then?" Jesus answered, "You say rightly that I am a king. For this cause I was born, and for this cause I have come into the world, that I should bear witness to the truth. Everyone who is of the truth hears my voice."

Pilate said to him, "What is truth?" And when he had said this, he went out again to the Jews, and said to them, "I find no fault in him at all."

John 19:9-12

And *Pilate* went again into the Praetorium, and said to Jesus, "Where are you from?" But Jesus gave him no answer. Then, Pilate said to him, "Are you not speaking to me? Do You not know that I have power to crucify you, and power to release you?"

Jesus answered, "You could have no power at all against me unless it had been given you from above. Therefore, the one who delivered me to you has the greater sin." From then on Pilate sought to release him, but the Jews cried out, saying, "If you let this man go, you are not Caesar's friend. Whoever makes himself a king speaks against Caesar."

ARE YOU THE KING?

Here, the Bible zooms in and gives us a tight shot of the conversation between Pilate and Jesus. Pilate asks Jesus, "Are you the King of the Jews?" Traditional expectations of Messiah entailed the belief that Christ, when he came, would overthrow the Romans and restore Jewish independence. Jewish leaders wanted to destroy Jesus, so they set him up within their own courts and sought his execution from the Roman courts by accusing him of claiming to be Messiah, an emerging *King of the Jews*, and, therefore, a direct threat to Caesar.

Jesus admits to Pilate that he is a king, but not in the sense in which the Jewish leaders, or Pilate, understand the term. He doesn't claim to be an *earthly* king, with warrior servants, but a heavenly king establishing a heavenly kingdom—the Kingdom of God.

WHAT IS TRUTH?

Jesus tells Pilate that he has come to bear witness of the truth. Pilate responds with a condescending rhetorical question—*What is truth?* This is a huge question, but Pilate intends it to dismiss the notion of truth altogether. Perhaps, had Pilate not asked the question in contempt, or derision, he might have gotten an answer. The possibility, accessibility and/or existence of absolute truth has long agitated the world, but Pilate asks the question and walks out without waiting for an answer.

Truth is relative to Pilate's situation. He doesn't care as much about philosophical questions of truth as he does about pragmatics, what works. *His truth* is that there is an angry mob outside his door, demanding that he put a man to death who has done nothing worthy of death. If he lets the man go, the *truth* is that he will have a riot on his hands and, possibly, lose his position as governor. If he puts Jesus to death, the *truth* will be that he has killed an innocent man. Pilate is looking for a solution, not a philosophy—not *truth*.

RELATIVE TRUTH

Many of us today care little for truth if it doesn't seem immediately relative to our circumstances. In this way, we're all a bit like Pilate. We want to know what works, and this isn't necessarily a bad thing. Truth requires relevance, application and just plain practicality as to how it relates to our lives. Pilate could have asked, "Truth? How does that help me now?"

There is truth. Truth is always relevant to practical life. The answers that we give to even the most tenuous philosophical questions about ultimate truth affect the choices that we make on a daily basis. Those who claim to value pragmatics over philosophy, are, whether they know it or not, actually saying, "I have already answered the most important philosophical questions about reality; all I need to know, now, is how to live those out." (You may want to read that again...) A good many decisions that a person makes throughout his or her day is made in light of the answers that the heart has knowingly or unknowingly already given to ultimate questions of being.

1. Is there a Creator/God?
2. Can he be known?
3. Has he revealed himself? What is he like?
4. Does he have a purpose in creation?
5. Does my life have purpose and meaning?
6. Is there life after death?
7. Will we be judged?

The answer to whether there is or isn't a God is not a matter of opinion, as if there is such a thing as *your truth* versus *my truth*. It is a point of fact. He either does exist or he doesn't exist. The answer is, however, beyond scientific verification. Our answer is a philosophical starting point, affecting every aspect of our life. Truth is not relative; it is absolute. We merely find ourselves unable to secure absolute certainty; we all gamble our souls, therefore, on our beliefs.

When Jesus says to Pilate, "I came to bear witness to the truth," he is not speaking of facts in regard to his case, but is declaring the existence of absolute truth, his knowledge of it, and his function in its regard. Jesus is the affirmative answer to the most foundational questions of life. He is the great YES to the most important questions of existence. Through his life and ministry Jesus says:

1. Yes, there is a God and I am he.
2. Yes, I have made him known.
3. Yes, he is revealed in me.
4. Yes, creation has a purpose; I have revealed it and am fulfilling it.
5. Yes, your life has purpose and meaning; I have revealed it and am fulfilling it.
6. Yes, there is life after death.... been there, done that.
7. Yes, God will judge every soul... but I have provided a path through judgment. "I am the way, the truth, and the life. No one comes to the Father except through me." (John 14:6)

LIFE APPLICATIONS:

1. Do you see truth as relative or absolute? Explain your reasons.

_____

_____

_____

_____

_____

_____

_____

_____

_____

2. Go through the seven questions of existence asked above and answer each of them to the best of your ability. Explain each answer and why you believe it.

_____

_____

_____

_____

_____

_____

_____

_____

_____

3. Explain the relationship between the answers that you give to those questions and the way you choose to live your life daily.

_____

_____

_____

_____

_____

_____

_____

_____

_____

_____

4. What do these words of Christ mean to you? "I am the way, the truth, and the life. No one comes to the Father except through me." (John 14:6)

_____

_____

_____

_____

_____

_____

_____

_____

_____

25

THE PROBLEM WITH PILATE

Luke 23:4-17

So Pilate said to the chief priests and the crowd, "I find no fault in this man." But they were the more fierce, saying, "He stirs up the people, teaching throughout all Judea, beginning from Galilee to this place."

When Pilate heard of Galilee he asked if the man were a Galilean. And as soon as he knew that he belonged to Herod's jurisdiction, he sent him to Herod, who was also in Jerusalem at that time. Now when Herod saw Jesus, he was exceedingly glad; for he had desired for a long *time* to see him, because he had heard many things about him, and he hoped to see some miracle done by him. Then, he questioned him with many words, but he answered him nothing. And the chief priests and scribes stood and vehemently accused him. Then, Herod, with his men of war, treated him with contempt and mocked him, arrayed him in a gorgeous robe, and sent him back to Pilate. That very day Pilate and Herod became friends with each other, for previously they had been at enmity with each other.

Then, Pilate, when he had called together the chief priests, the rulers, and the people, said to them, "You have brought this man to me, as one who misleads the people. And indeed, having examined him in your presence, I have found no fault in this man concerning those things of which you accuse him; no, neither did Herod, for I sent you back to him; and indeed nothing deserving of death has been done by him. I will therefore chastise him and release him," (for it was necessary for him to release one to them at the feast).

Matthew 27:16-18

At that time they had a notorious prisoner called Barabbas. Therefore, when they had gathered together, Pilate said to them, "Whom do you want me to release to you? Barabbas, or Jesus who is called Christ?" For he knew that they had handed him over because of envy.

John 18:40

Then, they all cried, saying, "Not this man, but Barabbas."

Matthew 27:19

While he was sitting on the judgment seat, his wife sent to him, saying, "Have nothing to do with that just man, for I have suffered many things today in a dream because of him."

PRAGMATISM

This song in the SAVIOR Musical was designed to create a dark, introspective atmosphere, listening to Pilate's mind while he tries to make a decision regarding Christ. He is faced with a stressful, yet vital, choice. He is torn between several conflicting voices, not the least of which is his own convictions about right and wrong. Indeed, his mental process relates to us and our own decision-making dilemmas.

Like many of us, Pilate was a pragmatist. *Pragmatism* stresses practical consequences as the essential basis for determining meaning, truth, or value. Pilate, however, was not only a practical guy; he was self-seeking. The consequences that mattered most were those that affected him directly. As he stands next to Jesus, you can almost feel the contrast. Pilate is a non-religious, non-Jew, a man of position, heavily swayed by both the expectations of his superiors and by popular opinion... he was a politician, after all. Jesus presents a real problem for Pilate, who is looking for a solution that sates his conscience, while protecting him from the manifold consequences of provoking a riot. There is no solution... something has to give.

SEARCHING FOR COMPROMISE

Pilate sees himself in a *lose-lose* situation, and he tries his best to get out of it. First, he tries to pass the buck by sending Jesus to Herod, in hopes that Herod will make the decision for him. King Herod, however, only wanted to see Jesus do some parlor tricks, probably in the nature of, *can you make this thingy disappear?* Upon realizing that Jesus was no threat, Herod sends him back to Pilate. Strike one—Herod only makes Pilate's decision harder by also finding Jesus innocent.

Pilate then tries to appeal to the sensibilities of the people using Barabbas. The Jews held a tradition at the time that the Romans allow one prisoner to be released on Passover. So Pilate tries to free Jesus: "Okay, folks, you can have me release this guy, this great guy, who really hasn't done anything wrong, who heals your sick, raises your dead, performs miracles… or I can release this murderous seditious scum bag…" *These Jewish leaders only turned Jesus over because They're jealous, certainly the people won't leave him to die.* Strike two—the people call for Barabbas. Pilate is running out of options.

Pilate then tries to appease the people, saying that he will beat Jesus and release him. Strike three—the people still call out for Barabbas. Pilate is realizing that there is no easy way out. He has to decide either for Christ, or against him. Then, something strange happens. He gets a warning from him wife, who has had a disturbing dream about Jesus.

Dreams were highly valued in the ancient world among Greeks, Romans and Jews alike, as vehicles for divine interaction. It is no small matter that Pilate's wife, troubled in a dream about Jesus, regards it as a warning. I believe Matthew's gospel records this incident as a way of illustrating Pilate's own conscience. The Bible says that by the witness of two or three let a thing be established; there are now three witnesses to the innocence of Christ vying for Pilate's attention: Herod, Pilate's own conscience, and now his wife's dream—have nothing to do with that just man.

SITTING IN THE JUDGMENT SEAT

Here is Pontius Pilate, sitting on the *judgment seat*, (of all places) wracking his brain, thumbing through his options, trying to judge between doing what's expedient, and what's right. Here he is, here's how the voices in his head may have sounded:

> *There's nothing wrong with this man. Herod is right, my wife is right—he is innocent.*
> *What shall I do?*
> *Someone tell me... Someone help me!*
> *I don't want to condemn an innocent man.*
> *Why should I choose this man's fate?*
> *I can appeal to Rome.*
> *I can't appeal to Rome—they will see me as a weak leader.*
> *I'll set him free, he is not guilty.*
> *If I let him go, the people may riot. If I have a riot, Rome may remove me from my post.*
> *What shall I do, someone tell me!*

It's pretty loud inside his head. The only decisions left are hard ones. There is no way out for Pilate. He has to make a decision. Either he's going to release Jesus, or kill him.

THINK ABOUT YOUR THINKING

We too sit in Pilate's judgment seat. Some, like Pilate, may have examined the case for Christ,[iv] but want nothing to do with him, as if failing to make a decision relieves us of responsibility. You can pardon the reference, but the band, Rush, said it right in their song Freewill: "If you choose not to decide, you still have made a choice." To "make no choice" is to choose against Christ.

Even those who once made the great choice of becoming a disciple of Christ, face the dilemma of choosing for him every day in the face of a crowd of conflicting voices, temptations and wise and foolish options. Discipleship is a struggle, and the first battle is in the mind. We, like Pilate, often know what we ought to do, what Christ would want us to do, but when under pressure, a chorus of voices invade the mind. A tension emerges between:

- Spiritual Voices: conscience, Scripture, conviction, moral standards, etc.

- Pragmatic Voices: like fear of loss, desire for gain, self-preservation, pleasure, etc.

- Popular Voices: like peer/cultural/community expectations, fear of man, desire for acceptance, etc.

Consider Pilate, pulled between his own conscience and his wife's dream on one end and the threat of riot from the populace and the fear of loss that this threat provokes on the other. In these moments, these times of pressure between doing what is right and doing what's pragmatic and doing what's popular, before you stand to make your decision, sit down in the Judgment Seat and think about your choices. Rather than reacting without thought, out of base impulses, stop and think.

New England Drivers' Ed trainers teach this acronym for rapid decision-making and I'll leave it here with you: IPDE—Identify, Predict, Decide, Execute.

- Identify the voices. What are the *spiritual* voices saying, what are the *pragmatic* voices saying, what are the *popular* voices saying?
- Predict the outcomes. Wisdom sees the end from the beginning. If you think you are the exception to the rule, think again.
- Decide what choice fits the kind of life you want to live; what decision will shape you into the kind of person you want to be? Every decision is a road somewhere.
- Execute your decision.

Every situation is different, posing its own set of challenges. Some situations afford us the time to contemplate the right course of action, while others do not. Though the pressure to decide for or against Christ was great, Pilate had time to weigh his decision, choosing to yield to one pressure or another. We need wisdom; sometimes pragmatic and popular voices speak truth, but, often, they color our inclinations; the more we accustom ourselves to distinguishing these voices, the easier it will become to make spiritually responsible decisions on the fly. The more we ignore spiritual voices, the quieter they become, weakening our consciences. Beyond all things seemingly practical, above the voice of the crowd, hear the voice of the Lord.

LIFE APPLICATIONS:

1. If you have made a decision to become a disciple of Christ, or are struggling with this decision, describe the inner dialogue that came, or is coming from the three different voices that we've discussed—spiritual, pragmatic, popular.

_____

_____

_____

_____

_____

_____

_____

_____

_____

2. Sometimes it is easy to know which voice is which; sometimes it is hard to know, especially under pressure and temptation. How can you better discern the voice of the Lord above the crowd, above what may seem immediately practical, or self-preserving in these hard moments?

_____

_____

_____

_____

_____

_____

_____

_____

_____

3. What does "sitting in the judgment seat" mean to you when you are under pressure to make a decision for Christ whether an initial embrace of Jesus as Lord, or the many ongoing choices we make as his disciples in a complex world?

_____

_____

_____

_____

_____

_____

_____

_____

_____

4. Would you describe your usual decision making process as more instinctual, or thoughtful? Explain. What are some practical things a person might do to transform over time to become more thoughtful in his or her decision making, to regularly implement IPDE?

_____

_____

_____

_____

_____

_____

_____

_____

_____

<h1 style="text-align: center;">26</h1>

<h2 style="text-align: center;">CRUCIFY HIM!</h2>

Matthew 27:22

Pilate said to them, "What then shall I do with Jesus who is called Christ?" And the multitude cried out, *"Crucify him!"*

John 19:1; Matthew 27:27-30

So then Pilate took Jesus and *scourged* him. Then, the soldiers of the governor took Jesus into the Praetorium and gathered the whole band of soldiers around him. And they stripped him and put a scarlet robe on him. When they had twisted a crown of thorns, they put *it* on his head, and a reed in his right hand. And they bowed the knee before him and mocked him, saying, "Hail, King of the Jews!" Then, they spat on him, and took the reed and struck him on the head.

SURROUNDED BY THE ENEMY

When I was about 16, I took the biggest beating of my life. I was playing guitar in a band with no name, hanging in a rough part of town, partying hard, being stupid. At one party, I was trying to impress some girl, while some other, much older, drunken fool tried to mock me. Though inebriated myself, I was a bit quicker on the uptake and verbally humiliated the guy, somehow intimidating him into backing down in front of everyone. He said he'd deal with me when he was sober, and he left. I woke up the next morning with immediate regret. *What did I do? He could have killed me...*

Weeks later, I was at a 4th of July bon fire in a park in that same rough part of town. Standing with some friends, I heard a guy say, *"Cashman? Oh, tell me that's not you?"* I turned to see a fist flying from the darkness. I dodged it and ended up grappling with its owner on the ground. He turned out to be a close friend to the guy I'd humiliated, and he fought dirty. He even bit me! I fought as hard as I could and he eventually cried uncle, but I was scraped up, half-drunk, chewed and totally exhausted.

When the fight ended, I limped off, to find my friends just in time to hear another voice calling from the shadows. I tried to run, but was too depleted from my brawl. As I reached the basketball courts, another friend of Sir Humiliated caught up to me. He rushed me, saying, "Hey man, come here, I want to talk to you," backing me against the court's chain link fence as his own personal cheering squad caught up.

I mustered up a rather pitiful spin kick, and he proceeded to beat me mercilessly. He proved an even dirtier fighter than the other guy. He bit my face, scratched me, pulled my hair, punched me several million times in the face for over an hour, all the while taunting my helplessness. My nightmare was the crowd's entertainment. I remember thinking, *Where are my friends? How am I going to get out of this?* When the guy finally let up, I gave one final lurch of dignity at his feet. Irritated, he stepped back and kicked me square in the face with his boot. At least it was over.

I stumbled to my feet and through the crowd, leaving my blood and pride all over that park, and began a long staggering walk through a maze of dark foreign streets, trying to find my friend's house; he wasn't there, but judging by the shocked look on his sister's face, I must have looked hideous. When I saw myself in the mirror through half-shut eyes, I was unrecognizable. Oh! and did I mention, completely humiliated.

That night was one of the worst nights of my life, but all that I endured does not even begin to compare to the suffering that awaited Christ in Pilate's court.

THE SCOURGING

Pilate, in his weakness, gave in to the pressure of the people. In an attempt to appease them, he had Jesus, a man whose innocence he had already declared, scourged. Scourging needed no introduction; the word carried its own horrors. If you've ever seen Mel Gibson's *Passion of the Christ*, then you'll understand why.

Scourging was a fierce beating with lictors' rods, or whips, called scorpions—leather straps with leaden balls, hooks, sharp spikes or shards of bone fixed into the ends. It brought a man to within an inch of his life, shredding his torso front and back, and rending his face beyond recognition. A whole band of soldiers (Some 400-600 men)[v] gathered in the inner hall for the occasion, finishing off Jesus' scourging with a mock coronation ceremony.[vi] They adorned this royal pretender with a crown of thorns, a robe, and a make-believe scepter, which they snatched from him, beating him in the head. They bowed, spit, punched and cruelly mocked him. I have seen the *Passion of the Christ* many times, but I don't think I've watched it once without crying at some part of the scourging scene. Beaten, yes, but more than that. He was abandoned, betrayed, humiliated, demeaned, falsely accused, and rejected by his own people. I find it overwhelming to imagine that he did all this, having the power to stop it, in order to lay down his life for his enemies!

FAMILIAR WITH SUFFERING

Following Christ does not exempt a person from suffering. Anyone who tells you otherwise is either lying or trying to sell you something. In fact, being a Christian often adds to your common share in human trouble, the anguish of struggling against sin, and the contempt of a world that glorifies wickedness. Suffering comes from without and from within; we all face various struggles in life.

- Physical: sickness, abuse, injury, poverty, etc.

- Emotional: depression, grief, frustration, rejection, self-condemnation, etc.

- Spiritual: struggle in the fight against sin, resisting the spirit of worldliness, spiritual warfare, etc.

The important thing to which we must cling in our souls is that we are not alone in any of our suffering, be it common or Christian. Isaiah 53:3 predicted that the Servant, Christ, would be "a man of sorrows, and familiar with suffering." Being "familiar with suffering" himself means that Christ can empathize with those who suffer.

When we suffer the unimaginable, it is a great temptation to think that God and Christ have forsaken us. How could he allow my spouse, my child, my parent, friend, or sibling to die? How could he allow my physical body, or those that I love, to suffer such injury or sickness? How could he expect me to maintain my faith when enduring such financial or emotional ruin? How long does he expect me to suffer, in this misery?

To say that Jesus understands is not meant as a trite pat on the head to those languishing in emotional and physical torments. It is difficult to grasp, but Jesus' attendance to our suffering as a Lord who has himself suffered is a powerful reality. He has not forsaken us in our hour of pain, nor in our decade of pain.

- He has given us comfort through *community*. He given us his church, the family of God, if we will give ourselves to it even in our pain.

- He has given us comfort through *coaching*. His Word offers wisdom, hope, guidance, perspective and promise, if we will read and meditate on it.

- He has given us comfort through *communication*. Prayer is a vent into God's ever-listening ear, if we will pour out our hearts honestly to Christ.

- He has given comfort through *communion*. The Holy Spirit is literally called "The Comforter," he who comes along side us in our need.

Jesus knows. He gets it. He's been there, suffered that, and will never forsake you, even in your darkest days.

LIFE APPLICATIONS:

1. List some of your own most distinctive past or present personal sufferings that pushed you to the end of yourself and/or put your faith the test (physical, emotional, or spiritual).

_____

_____

_____

_____

_____

_____

_____

_____

_____

2. What does the sentence, "Jesus suffered for you," mean to you? Does thinking about the many things that Jesus suffered during his years among men give you any consolation or emotional comfort in your own suffering? Does it make you feel understood? If so, why? If not, why not?

_____

_____

_____

_____

_____

_____

_____

_____

_____

_____

3. Elaborate on the benefits of the comforts of Community, Coaching, Communication and Communion during times of suffering. Have they helped you? How?

_____

_____

_____

_____

_____

_____

_____

_____

_____

_____

_____

_____

_____

_____

_____

_____

_____

_____

_____

_____

_____

_____

27

HERE IS YOUR KING

John 19:4-15

Pilate then went out again, and said to them, "Behold, I am bringing him out to you, that you may know that I find no fault in him." Then, Jesus came out, wearing the crown of thorns and the purple robe. And Pilate said to them, "Behold the man!"

Therefore, when the chief priests and officers saw him, they cried out, saying, "Crucify him, crucify him!"

Pilate said to them, "You take him and crucify him, for I find no fault in him."

The Jews answered him, "We have a law, and according to our law, he ought to die, because he made himself the Son of God."

Therefore, when Pilate heard that saying, he was the more afraid, and went again into the Praetorium, and said to Jesus, "Where are you from?" But Jesus gave him no answer.

Then, Pilate said to him, "Are you not speaking to me? Do you not know that I have power to crucify you, and power to release you?"

Jesus answered, "You could have no power at all against me unless it had been given you from above. Therefore, the one who delivered me to you has the greater sin."

From then on Pilate sought to release him, but the Jews cried out, saying, "If you let this man go, you are not Caesar's friend. Whoever makes himself a king speaks against Caesar."

When Pilate therefore heard that saying, he brought Jesus out and sat down in the judgment seat in a place that is called The Pavement, but in Hebrew, Gabbatha. Now it was the Preparation Day of the Passover, and about the sixth hour. And he said to the Jews, "Behold your king!"

But they cried out, "Away with him, away with him! Crucify him!"

Pilate said to them, "Shall I crucify your king?"

The chief priests answered, "We have no king but Caesar!"

JESUS, BE WITH ME NOW

About a year before I came to Christ, I was at a friend's house, hanging out with him and his father. We were sitting around talking about the existence of God. They were both staunch atheists, and I had a basic belief in God. My friend's father asked me why I believed, so I told my story:

You may remember that I was a bit of a hockey puck in my parent's custody dispute when I was in the fourth grade. Upon the first day of attending a new Catholic school a kind woman teacher, told our class that if we were ever scared, we should say, "Jesus, be with me now." Seemed easy enough.

That night, I awoke in the throes of terror. My body was actually convulsing up and down on my bed. I'm still not sure why. I may have been having a seizure, reenacting a scene from *The Exorcist*, or just having a physical reaction to all the upheaval I was dealing with, but at the age of 9 or 10, I wasn't trying to analyze; I just repeated the kind teacher's words—"Jesus, be with me now. Jesus, be with me now…"

Then something extraordinary happened. It was as if someone threw a bucket of peace over my whole body. The fear melted away, and I was instantly calm. I didn't know anything about the Bible, or Jesus, or the gospel, but I knew Jesus was there in that room with me;

his spirit was palpable. From that point on, I believed in God.

In my telling that night to my friend and his father, I got no further than my recitation of *'Jesus, be with me now'* when my friend's father suddenly started screaming, "Shut up, Shut-up! SHUT....UP!!!" Then, he insulted me, berated me and belittled the very idea of God. I was shocked. I didn't know what to say. He had always been kind to me. He made no apologies, gave no explanation. *What did I say?* I wondered.

The answer—I said good things about his enemy. I began to realize that there was real hatred for Christ in the world. Like Pilate, I recognized it, but didn't understand it. I was like a third party observer, convinced in Jesus' innocence in this regard, but uncommitted to him personally.

A WAR OF WORLDS

Pilate looks on in frustrated bewilderment at the Jewish religious leaders' determination to kill an innocent man. He was witnessing a great battle, unaware of the nature of the war... a war of worlds—The Kingdom of God versus The Kingdom of this World. William Law says, "The history of the gospel is chiefly the history of Christ's conquest over the spirit of the world."[vii]

The spirit of the world, often called merely, "The World," concerns the prevailing essence of human inclination—its mindset, desires, passions, tempers, and all of its standards and values. The Apostle John summarizes the *spirit of the world*, saying, "The whole world lies in wickedness," (1 John 5:19) "For all that is in the world, the lust of the flesh, and the lust of the eyes, and the pride of life are not of the Father, but is of the world." (John 2:16) So a spiritual war of light over darkness is waging and this moment in the gospel is one of its greatest battles. Pilate is caught in the crossfire.

LIGHT HAS COME INTO THE WORLD

I think we'd all agree that there is something wrong with the world. What many do not know, however, is what is *specifically* wrong with the world. What's wrong with the world is the "spirit of the world," that prevailing bent toward wickedness sweeping every human society along like debris in a raging river. This river does not run of its own natural accord, however, but is driven along by yet darker forces. Satan as both an entity and a category has waged a war against God's rule by way of destroying that which God loves best—humanity. This is not a struggle between equals, but, having lured humanity into his own rebellion against God and God's ways, Satan has been granted a temporary status among us. As the "god of this world," he seeks to blind the minds of unbelievers to the light of the gospel. (2 Corinthians 4:4) He seduces hearts already darkened by sin with the essence of "Do what thou wilt,"—Satanism's code of law.[viii] Paul says of our interaction with him, "And you were dead in the trespasses and sins in which you once walked, following the course of this world, following the prince of the power of the air, the spirit that is now at work in the sons of disobedience—among whom we all once lived in the passions of our flesh, carrying out the desires of the body and the mind, and were by nature children of wrath, like the rest of mankind. (Ephesians 2:1-3) The world, driven on by satanic forces and human rebellion, is lost in darkness, but the light of the Spirit of Christ has broken into that darkness.

The painful conflict between light and darkness is the provocation to the war of worlds to which Pilate was a grand witness, and I, to a lesser degree. There can be no peace between God and *the spirit of the world.* "God is light and in him is no darkness at all." (1 John 1:5) In Jesus, "light has come into the world, and men loved darkness rather than light, because their deeds were evil. For everyone practicing evil hates the light..." (John 3:19-20) "He was in the world, and the world was made through him, and the world did not know him." (John 1:9-10)

It is easy, in a media driven world to fall victim to a sweeping prescriptivism, a "So I believe and so must you also," tone that tells you in every commercial, TV show, movie, talk show and song that anyone whose anyone thinks "this way" about life. The higher calling of God and Christ by both Word and Spirit is often in direct opposition to these voices.

This conflict may be unavoidable, but God does not hate those in the world. Rather, as John says, "God so loved the world, that he gave his only Son, that whoever believes in him should not perish but have eternal life." (John 3:16) He also says, "In him was life, and the life was the light of men. The light shines in the darkness, and the darkness has not overcome it." (John 1:4-5) "And we have seen and testify that the Father has sent his son to be the SAVIOR of the world." (1 John 4:14) Jesus is warring *for* those in the world, and we are with him in the fight. In this war, there is no neutral. The religious leaders chose their king; they chose their side, so must we.

LIFE APPLICATIONS:

1. Do you perceive the spiritual war to which so many scriptures allude? Describe it. Can you see your place in it? Describe it.

_____

_____

_____

_____

_____

_____

_____

_____

_____

_____

2. In your own words, describe what is meant by *the spirit of the world.* What are the directions of its influences? (i.e. What is *the world* like?)

_____

_____

_____

_____

_____

_____

_____

_____

_____

_____

3. Give some general examples of the tension between *the spirit of the world* and *the Spirit of Christ?*

_____

_____

_____

_____

_____

_____

_____

_____

_____

_____

4. In what ways have you been influenced by the *spirit of the world,* the spirit of "Do what thou wilt?" In what areas of your personal life do you perceive the most tension between worldly influence and Godly influence?

_____

_____

_____

_____

_____

_____

_____

_____

_____

_____

28

CRUCIFY HIM! CRUCIFY HIM!

John 19:12-15

From then on Pilate sought to release him, but the Jews cried out, saying, "If you let this man go, you are not Caesar's friend. Whoever makes himself a king speaks against Caesar.

When Pilate therefore heard that saying, he brought Jesus out and sat down in the judgment seat in a place that is called The Pavement, but in Hebrew, Gabbatha. Now it was the Preparation Day of the Passover, and about the sixth hour. And he said to the Jews, "Here is your King!"

The chief priests answered, "We have no king but Caesar!"

Luke 23:20-21

Pilate, therefore, wishing to release Jesus, again called out to them. But they shouted, saying, "Crucify him, crucify him!"

JESUS WALKS INTO A BAR

The Bible calls us ambassadors for Christ. Ambassadors from an enemy nation are often treated *as* the enemy. Even enemy embassy buildings take it on the chin in a time of war, because, of course, a friend of an enemy is an enemy.

After I graduated Bible College, I started a Christian band called,

"The Way," with Dave (my friend who brought me to Christ). In hopes of bringing the gospel into places where we'd be… effective, our manager got us, and another Christian group, a gig in a bar outside of Providence. We arrived as the other group was finishing their set, and the bar owner was fuming that he'd gotten Christian bands for the night. Then, the owner snapped, "Are you guys a Christian band?"

"Yes, we are," I said as politely as I could.

"Well, you're not playing tonight."

"Ok."

"Your manager didn't tell me you guys were a Christian band."

"All of the information on us was in the package we sent you. Did you get..."

"Yeah, I got it," he snarled, cutting me off, "I didn't read it." My band stood wide-eyed in the distance as he tore into me.

"Man, I'm sorry you're just finding this out, but we're pretty good," I whimsied, smiling, trying to bring a little levity into the conversation.

"Listen, this is a bar room," he said, building into a tirade (I was glad he clarified) "And this is a *whiskey* drinking crowd!!!" He was getting pretty worked up, but he suddenly stopped; then his countenance changed. "Alright, look, you can go on," he said, but you're not going to get paid. And if I hear anything I don't like, I'll shut you off!"

"That's fine," I said in amazement. Then, we went on.

The bar crowd was actually into the music, but, as soon as we finished, the owner cranked a Rage Against the Machine song at the back bar, and hollered along with the lyrics, "[the heck with] you, I won't do what you tell me!" Then, the whole rear of the bar started chanting the line as loud as they could in obvious defiance to our message and our God. It continued to grow rowdier and uglier, and we actually thought that they might physically attack us as we packed up… tough crowd.

Dave's wife, Shelby, walked up to the owner as we hurriedly pulled our stuff together and asked him why he was so upset. "They're a Christian band!" he yelled, "This is a bar! Christian bands belong in a church, not a bar!"

Now, he had a point, perhaps, but our band believed that God opened a door for us to play there. To this effect, Shelby's exact reply was, "Jesus sent them here."

It was a bold sentiment and apparently the owner thought so too, because he jumped over the bar, got in her face and shouted in a fit of anger, "Well nobody here wants to get saved!"

In her calm Shelby-like manner, she asked, "How do you know?"

The guy turned around and, at the top of his lungs, shouted, "DOES ANYONE HERE WANT TO GET SAVED?" The people started getting ugly and rambunctious again, a few people left in a hurry. One older gentleman in the back stood up and said something like:

"You guys are crazy! You're all going to hell! I'm not having anything to do with this!" At that, the man walked out. Christian or not, the man noticed something. He witnessed the world's hatred of Christ. We, at least in part, experienced it. On a rolling wave of anger, they swept us out the door, slammed it and locked it behind us.

CAESAR'S PAL

Hatred is a strong word, but it's safe to say that the Jews hated Rome and hated everything about the Roman presence among them. It is beyond ironic, therefore, when they accuse Pilate, saying, "If you let this man go, you are not Caesar's friend. Whoever makes himself a king speaks against Caesar." and "We have no king, but Caesar!" Their hatred for Jesus was so deep, that they would rather claim friendship and submission to a pagan ruler, than to allow Jesus to live in their midst. In the confrontation between light and darkness provoked by Jesus' incarnation, they choose darkness. "We have no king, but Caesar!"

For Pilate to associate with Jesus, by merely permitting him life, he makes himself their enemy and Caesar's enemy. James, the brother of Jesus, expresses the tension well if in opposite terms. "Don't you know that the *friendship* of the world is enmity with God?" Whosoever will be a friend of the world is an enemy of God." (James 4:4) So, by default, he who makes himself a friend of God becomes the world's enemy.

HATRED OF THE WORLD

Christ said, "If the world hates you, you know that it hated me before *it hated* you. If you were of the world, the world would love its own. Yet because you are not of the world, but I chose you out of the world, therefore the world hates you." (John 15:18-19) Remember, "The World" is the spirit and mindset that prevails over humanity with all of its standards and values. It is at enmity with God; therefore, those caught up in it display a form of hatred for God and for those who are associated with him, embodying his rule.

It is easy to forget, living in a culture that has been so heavily influenced by Christianity and its values that we live in the same fallen world as Christ did, the same world that crucified him. The world become a friend is a more seductive enemy. The appearance of acceptance, tolerance and politeness can be more insidious, more dangerous to our hearts than open hostility. It blinds us to the reality of the battle. It weakens our resolve to fight for our souls and for the souls of others. The *spirit of the world* will always be opposed to Christ. If the Spirit of Christ lives in you, and you attempt to advance his kingdom, then you too will experience the world's hatred of him. This is not to say that every non-Christian hates every Christian. It is to say that at a base level the Spirit of Christ stands opposed to the current and the nature of the spirit of this world. Those caught up in it often find themselves fighting the Spirit of Christ in the Christian, and, even more frequently, fighting the biblical standards that Christians strive to maintain.

VOICES

That night my band played at the bar, we experienced hatred for Christ first hand. Those people couldn't have hated us personally;

they didn't know us enough to hate us. They hated who we represented; we were ambassadors of their enemy in a perpetual spiritual war. As those mobs before Pilate demanded that he crucify Jesus to prove himself their friend and Caesar's friend, so a host of voices can still be heard giving that battle cry, "Crucify him! Crucify him!" They demand from each of us, sometimes with a shout, sometimes with a seductive whisper, that we crucify Christ from our hearts, crucify him from our minds, crucify him from our lives! It is not personal; it is spiritual. Though this seldom makes us feel better when we are the one in the crosshairs, being armed with this knowledge helps us to avoid personal offense and better prepares us to respond wisely and redemptively to it.

LIFE APPLICATIONS:

1. Based on what you've read in this chapter, how do you perceive the spiritual struggle between this world order and Christ? Do you believe this hatred even exists? Why or why not.

_____

_____

_____

_____

_____

_____

_____

_____

_____

_____

2. Give some examples of times that you have witnessed hostility toward you or others for the sake of God, or godliness?

_____

_____

_____

_____

_____

_____

_____

_____

_____

_____

3. In what areas of your life do you hear the *threatening* voices calling you to crucify Christ from your life? In what areas of your life do you hear the *seductive* voices calling you to crucify Christ from your life?

_____

_____

_____

_____

_____

_____

_____

_____

_____

4. Does knowing the source of persecution take the personal sting out of it for you? Does it engender more tender and sympathetic feelings toward those trapped in the spirit of the world, opposing the Spirit of Christ? Explain.

_____

_____

_____

_____

_____

_____

_____

_____

29

HE'S JUST A MAN

Matthew 27:20-23

But the chief priests and elders persuaded the multitudes that they should ask for Barabbas and destroy Jesus. The governor answered and said to them, "Which of the two do you want me to release to you?"

They said, "Barabbas!"

And the governor said, "Why, what evil hath he done?"

But they cried out the more, saying, "Let him be crucified."

JESUS CHRIST SUPERSTAR

I was teaching music lessons at the time when writing SAVIOR. A student came to me with a song from Jesus Christ Superstar that she wanted to learn. It was a song from Mary Magdalene's perspective that included the line, "He's just a man." It was apparently the author's intention to show that Mary M. may have had a romantic interest with Jesus. When I heard it, I thought, Okay, that's an interesting response, neat line, but, perhaps, the wrong context. I thought it would be better coming from Pilate and the crowd. Here, this SAVIOR song breaks the heavy musical mood as Pilate tries to interrupt and appeal to the crowd, "He's Just a Man!" He says, "People can't you hear what you are saying?" It's as if he's pleading with them, "He's just a man, why should I kill him?" Then they reply, "He's just a man, so kill him!" He feels like he's missing something important. The entire dynamic of the conflict between Jesus and the people is lost on Pilate.

WHY?

To the crowd's incessant chants for Jesus' execution, Pilate asks this obvious question—"Why, what evil has he done?" (Matthew 27:23) It seemed crazy to Pilate that these men would want Jesus killed... especially after he was so brutally scourged and beaten. "Why?" He asked. It's a great question. I'm not sure if he ever got his answer. I'm not sure the crowd could have even answered the question for themselves. He is trying to reason with the unreasonable. Pilate is looking at the situation from a point of justice and injustice. On the surface, Jesus did nothing deserving of death; he finds no fault in him. Beneath the surface, a war of worlds is waging—the Kingdom of God versus the Kingdom of Darkness. He is thrust into the battle and forced to choose a side.

UNREASONABLE

You don't have to be a Christian to see the irrationality and the effects of this war, even today. To the thinking man, there is no sensibility to the battles, no natural reason for the enmity, no facts behind the propaganda, no logic behind the gross hatred of Christ and his followers. Christians, as a whole, while always open to the accusation of being hypocrites, while always falling short of Christ's perfection, do, at least, strive as a community to be the best version of themselves, to love, to show charity, to check their own selfishness, to curb lust, anger, hatred, rage, jealousy, envy, and the like. Call them intolerant, or fanatical but why all the hatred? The problems within the church, while real, are *statistically* nothing compared to the vileness outside the church.

This hatred is not based on reason, or philosophy or logic, or misinformation, and cannot be overcome by these alone. This hatred comes from the confrontation of divine light with hearts darkened by sin and rebellion and can only be overcome by the yielding of one's will to the will of Christ.

THE POWER OF PERSUASION

At Rhode Island college, I took a Logic course. They had us study various false forms of arguments called fallacies. These fallacies were given weird Latin names. There was one in the bunch called an *Ad Populum*. An *Ad Populum* asserts falsely, that consensus equals truth. It alleges that, "If many believe so, then it *is* so. It is going along with the crowd, getting with the program, going along to get along, 10,000 ants can't be wrong. Its power is the persuasion of popular opinion, the overwhelming allusion of truth, the threat of rocking the boat, and the rewards of belonging. Adolph Hitler used the Ad Populum incessantly to stir the German nation to war. The *Ad Populum* is where facts are displaced by hype and hysteria.

It is a powerful tool. Some in this crowd before Jesus, who were crying out, "Hosanna in the highest!" only a week before, were now persuaded to cry, "Crucify him!" Even Pilate was swept up in it, asking, "What then shall I do with Jesus who is called Christ?" Why was he asking the crowd what he, *the governor*, should do? Wasn't his decision to be based on justice, right and wrong and not on popular opinion? We have to be careful of what is persuading us, what is being prescribed by the world for us to believe and not believe and what voices are influencing our spiritual choices. We ought to be careful to ask this, "What shall I do?" question of God rather than of popular opinion.

REASONING WITH THE UNREASONABLE

Pilate, not understanding the nature of his situation, attempted to use reason to overcome a spiritual struggle. The confrontation of Christ with the sinful heart of an individual is always a spiritual struggle. It is easy for the church community to lose track of this when seeking to share the gospel. While externals like music styles, buildings, attractive programs, and loving encounters are not unimportant in the process of engaging the world around us, it always comes down in the end to a spiritual confrontation, a clashing of wills—God's versus Man's.

Understanding this endgame helps us in at least three ways.

1. The hatred of the world is not personal... it's spiritual. Even the most vicious God-hater needs Jesus and is an object of divine love. There are enough obstacles between people and Christ without us becoming one of them through personal offense, or being unnecessarily offensive.

2. People are the casualties in this war of the worlds. Internal and external forces are working to persuade them. A cacophony of voices assault their senses; a flood of worldly propaganda seeks to cloud their judgment. We are on a rescue mission from God, helping others to hear the voice of God above the crowd of voices persuading them away from him.

3. It reminds us to keep focused on the gospel message and not on manipulative or crafty methods of wooing an audience. If we perpetually compromise the gospel message, persuading people with style without substance, we may end up winning people to the community of the church and not to Jesus, himself.

In this War of the Worlds, we are not just voices of reason, but ambassadors for Christ. Our struggle in the world, to win those caught by the world, is not purely mental or physical; it is spiritual. The Apostle Paul says it this way:

"Now we have received, not the spirit of the world, but the Spirit who is from God, that we might know the things that have been freely given to us by God.

These things we also speak, not in words which man's wisdom teaches, but which the Holy Spirit teaches, comparing spiritual things with spiritual. But the natural man does not receive the things of the Spirit of God, for they are foolishness to him; nor can he know *them*, because they are spiritually discerned." (1 Corinthians 2:12-14)

LIFE APPLICATIONS:

1. Think of a time when you saw a Christian respond well to a negative reaction to his/her witness? Think of a time when the Christian responded poorly? Why do you suppose the responses differed?

_____

_____

_____

_____

_____

_____

_____

_____

_____

_____

_____

_____

_____

_____

_____

_____

_____

_____

_____

_____

2. How can you help people to hear the voice of God above the crowd of voices that persuade them away from God?

_____

_____

_____

_____

_____

_____

_____

_____

_____

_____

3. What are some methods used today that may win people to the church community, but not to Jesus himself? What are some ways to share the Word of God in a presentable manner without forsaking the message.

_____

_____

_____

_____

_____

_____

_____

_____

_____

_____

30

MY HANDS ARE CLEAN

Matthew 27:24-26a

When Pilate saw that he could not prevail at all, but rather that a tumult was rising, he took water and washed his hands before the multitude, saying, "I am innocent of the blood of this just person. You see to it." And all the people answered and said, "His blood be on us and on our children." Then, he released Barabbas to them.

Luke 23:24-25

So Pilate gave sentence that it should be as they requested. And he released to them the one they requested, who for rebellion and murder had been thrown into prison; but he delivered Jesus to their will.

THREE IRONIES

It is common for biblical characters to embody common human traits. We can easily see a bit of ourselves in the characters in this scene. In these characters and in their responses, we can see three great ironies collide at this final Pilate episode, in—the release of Barabbas, the final decision of Pilate, and the cries of the people.

BARABBAS

Barabbas is an *insurrectionist*, meaning that he has been imprisoned for attempting to overthrow Roman rule. He is also a murderer…

and a perfect picture of us. We could hardly design a better typology for the sinner's condition before Christ. Having rebelled against the rule of God, we are insurrectionists of the first order, deserving of the death sentence decreed against us before a holy God. We, like Barabbas, have received a pardon at the expense of the innocent— the guilty is set free while the innocent is condemned. It is interesting that, while Barabbas goes free, whose name literally means *son of the Father*, Jesus, the Son of God, dies, opening the paths of peace that all may become Sons of God.

BLAME SHIFTING

Barabbas becomes a type of scapegoat for Pilate's conscience. Having done "everything" he could to save Jesus, Pilate uses a tradition of prisoner release to give the crowds an opportunity to save him. There was this murderer, however, an insurrectionist, and the Jewish leaders convince the crowd to call for the release of this scoundrel, Barabbas, instead of Jesus. There is no doubt that Pilate could have released Jesus if he was willing to face the riotous consequences for doing so, but this demand for Barabbas defeats Pilate's resolve. He buckles to the pressure and to the threat, condemning Jesus to their will—death. Pilate, who has the power to save the innocent if he chooses, literally washes his hands of the matter. He who is finally responsible for Jesus' death, shirks responsibility in his own conscience, blaming the people. Wanting to exempt himself from the responsibility of making a decision about Jesus, he physically washes his hands in protest, establishing an ageless figure… "I wash my hands of it." His failure to choose for Jesus is a choice against Jesus.

In this, Pilate shows us that the human capacity for self-justification is almost immeasurable. We blame others for our failings as if, given what they have done, *we* had no other option but to sin. "They made me do it." "I am a victim, so it's not my fault." "What else was I supposed to do?" "I had to." "If you hadn't… then I wouldn't have…" These are common excuses for our poor choices, as if other people's sin justifies our own. We come by it honestly, however; Adam, the original blame shifter, showed us how. Within moments of becoming the father of all sinners, Adam blames both Eve and God himself for his own rebellion against God's law. He says, "The woman whom you gave to be with me, she gave me of the tree, and I ate." (Genesis 3:12)

HIS BLOOD BE ON US

The third great irony in this episode comes to Pilate by way of the people whom he blames for Jesus' condemnation. They are ultimately responsible for Jesus' death, as Jesus himself says, "The one who handed me over to you has the greater sin." (John 19:11) They choose a murderous rebel, rather than a loving miracle worker, and grow increasingly threatening as Pilate attempts to release Jesus and appease their fury. Even Jesus' ravaged body does nothing to sate their bloodlust; they cry out for his crucifixion. Here, as Pilate futilely seeks to wash his hands of his own responsibility, a stain that cannot be removed with water, the people welcome their guilt with exuberance. Insensible to the accidental double entendre of their own cries, they shout, "His blood be on us and on our children." Indeed, even in the midst of their darkest hour, Jesus is ready to shed his blood for them. Paul says it well, "God demonstrates his own love toward us, in that while we were still sinners, Christ died for us. Much more then, having now been justified by his blood, we shall be saved from wrath through him." (Romans 5:8-9)

HUMANITY ON PARADE

In this chapter, we witness a kind of humanity on parade, as ironies collide in these final moments of Jesus' trial before Pilate. We can see something of ourselves in these characters—Barabbas, Pilate and the people.

- We can see ourselves like Barabbas, guilty, deserving of any and every punishment God should choose to deliver, exchanged for an innocent man, who is here, remember, of his own accord, refusing angelic aid, human intervention, and divine right. We live because he died.

- We see ourselves making choices like Pilate, who refuses to embrace his own responsibility for Jesus' death. He had the power to deliver him, but allowed the sins of others to dictate his own behavior. He justifies his sin by blaming their pressure and not his weakness. Like Pilate, our failure to choose for Jesus is a choice against Jesus.

- Even so, we can be covered like the people, who in the midst of their own murderous rage against the Son of God become recipients of grace and mercy, benefiting from the blood that they shed, foreshadowed in the irony of their own words, "His blood be on us and on our children."

- We should be merciful like Christ, who showed mercy and grace to those around him even when they were murderously wrong.

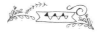

LIFE APPLICATIONS:

1. Can you see a fair comparison of your spiritual condition in Barabbas? Do you tend to assess your goodness based on a comparison with those around you? Do you imagine yourself more deserving of grace and mercy than Barabbas? Explain.

_____

_____

_____

_____

_____

_____

_____

_____

_____

2. Think about a time from your past when you have blamed others for your bad behavior or choices. Name some areas in your life now where you have a tendency to justify yourself. List some steps you might take to both remind yourself about your self-justifying patterns and to change the process while still in the midst of a situation.

_____

_____

_____

_____

_____

_____

_____

_____

3. Think of a time when you felt that you were shown mercy even when behaving badly… a time you were thankful that others responded graciously to you. How can keeping God's mercy to you (as a Barabbas) in mind help you be a more merciful person to others?

_____

_____

_____

_____

_____

_____

_____

_____

_____

_____

31

THE CRUCIFIXION

Luke 23:26-27

Now as they led him away, they laid hold of a certain man, Simon a Cyrenian, who was coming from the country, and on him they laid the cross that he might bear it after Jesus.

And a great multitude of the people followed him, and women who also mourned and lamented him. There were also two others, criminals, led with him to be put to death. And when they had come to the place called Calvary, there they crucified him.

Matthew 27:33-35

And when they had come to a place called Golgotha, that is to say, Place of a Skull, they gave him sour wine mingled with gall to drink. But when he had tasted *it,* he would not drink.

Then, they crucified him, and the criminals, one on the right hand and the other on the left—and divided his garments, casting lots, that it might be fulfilled which was spoken by the prophet:

They divided my garments among them, and for my clothing they cast lots.

CRUCIFIXION

Crucifixion is about as horrendous a death as anyone could suffer. Crucifixion is a slow, agonizing death that can take hours and often days. Jesus would have been stripped bare to increase his humiliation. He was nailed to a cross beam through his wrists and to a vertical beam through his ankles. He was propped upright, bringing all his weight down on the spikes holding him, unable to breathe without pushing up against them to take the weight off his already shredded torso. The victims of crucifixion would often contract hypothermia from exposure, causing constant shivering and convulsing; strength would wane as the agony increased, until they finally died.

In composing this song for SAVIOR, we tried to capture the violence of the act and the depravity of the hatred that led to it, which is exemplary of the ugliness of the sin that made it necessary in the first place. I knew the music needed to be heavy, but wanted also to give the vocals (the Roman soldiers) a sort of taunting, nanny-nah-nana-nah sound to them as they mocked him. This walk to the cross would have been an aggressive and forceful one, so the instrumental sections are in an obscure time signature to emulate a sort of pushing, unsettling feeling.

This is a dark moment in the gospel. Here we see Jesus as his scourged body struggles to carry a heavy wooden cross. He can hear the laments and cries of the women who loved him, mingled with the jeering voices of others who scorned him. Roman soldiers push him along that long walk outside of the city to Golgotha, that hill they called the Place of the Skull where he would ultimately be crucified.

CRUCIFIED WITH CHRIST

Prior to giving my life to Christ, I didn't understand how Christ being crucified on a cross 2,000 years ago affected my life at all. It was an historical event meant to teach us that God loves us and would suffer to show us that love. I gave no more than a periodic pause to think, *That was nice of God.* For me, the change in my thinking came with a change in my heart; I experienced the power of the cross, as I embraced a new vision of the reality of God and of his purpose for my existence. It changed my life.

There are many aspects of Jesus' death that need to be considered, but, here, I'd like to discuss the importance of crucifixion as a recurring metaphor in Scripture for our commitment to and our association with Jesus and our resulting struggle with sin as a disciple of Christ.

- Jesus said, "Whoever wants to be my disciple must deny themselves and take up their cross and follow me." (Mark 8:34)

- The Apostle Paul uses this picture repeatedly. "Knowing this, that our *old man* was crucified with him, that the body of sin might be done away with, that we should no longer be slaves of sin." (Romans 6:6)

- "I have been *crucified with Christ;* it is no longer I who live, but Christ lives in me; and the *life* which I now live in the flesh I live by faith in the Son of God, who loved me and gave himself for me." (Galatians 2:20)

- "Those who are Christ's have *crucified the flesh* with its passions and desires." (Galatians 5:24)

- "For if you live according to the flesh, you will die; but if by the Spirit you put to death the misdeeds of the body, you will live." (Romans 8:13)

These are powerful scriptural metaphors, but their language can be difficult to grasp practically. What does it even mean, in a day to day sense, to be crucified with Christ, to put to death the misdeeds of the flesh by the Spirit? What does this actually look like... feel like? How does this affect our daily lives?

WHITE KNUCKLING IT

When we talk about crucifying the flesh, what do we imagine this struggle to be, even if we do understand that "flesh" means sinful passions and desires and not just physical being and strength. The very idea of simply stopping so many sinful behaviors can seem daunting, if not crazy and unrealistic. Images of a perpetual white knuckled suppression of unabated passions would scare any sensible person. What a dismal existence, to be always wanting, but never having, to be always in the throes of unmet desire; it sounds miserable. This is not what Jesus or Paul means by "crucifying the flesh daily."

THROUGH THE SPIRIT

There is a difference between suppression and crucifixion. Suppression leaves us fighting the "flesh" with the flesh, resisting temptations to do things that remain in our hearts as a viable option. "Crucifixion" with Christ is a spiritual defeat of sinful options altogether. It is not a calling to accomplish the same old job, robbed of the old tools, but is a call to do a new job with new tools and more than a little divine help and guidance. Imagine two competing scenarios.

In the 1ˢᵗ scenario, a person tells you to give up your present way of life to go live in a nation without technology of any kind. "For what purpose?" you ask. "Because it is the right way to live," he says. Most could not even imagine making such a choice. They like too many things about their life to even entertain it: movies, music, food, clothes, comforts, friends.

In the 2ⁿᵈ scenario, the person says, "I have a great mission for you. People in an undeveloped nation need your help. You will have to give up many things, but you will radically transform the lives of these people." This person shows you pictures of hurting people; your heart reaches out to them. Seeing them, you cannot turn away. You know that you may have bouts of longing for home, struggles over the things and people you left behind, adjustments to a new way of living, but you have replaced these with something more meaningful than the rat race, more noble than keeping up with the Joneses.

Taking up our cross to follow Christ is like this second option, but thinking about it from afar can feel like the first. Hebrews 12:2 describes this difference even for Jesus, who endured the cross, despising its shame "for the joy that was set before him… and sat down at the right hand of the throne of God."

In taking up our cross to follow Jesus, we embrace a path in life empowered by a grander vision and mission than anything we might have imagined when we lived only for our own self-gratification, only for our endless replication of the patterns that the world has given to us. God changes our hearts, enlarges our scope, empowers us by his Spirit, educates us through his Word, and hones us with his wisdom and discipline.

We are not merely called *from* something bad, but are also called *to* something great, and, for the joy set before us, we can endure our cross, as Jesus endured his. If we will set aside our past desires and accept what he desires for us, he fills our souls with a divine mission and seeks to fill our hearts and minds with a grand vision of what we can become in him, and what he can accomplish through us.

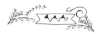

LIFE APPLICATIONS:

1. What does crucify the flesh through the Spirit, take up your cross and follow me, mean to you?

_____

_____

_____

_____

_____

_____

_____

_____

_____

_____

2. Give some examples from your life where you are, or have been, "white knuckling it" in suppressing sinful desires. How would or has "crucifying the flesh" look different in those same circumstances? What did or would have to change in your thinking to shift from one to the other?

_____

_____

_____

_____

_____

_____

_____

_____

_____

3. Have you experienced, through your relationship with Christ, a radical shift in your sense of purpose? Did this shift have an impact on particular sin issues in your life?

_____

_____

_____

_____

_____

_____

_____

_____

_____

_____

32

FATHER FORGIVE THEM

Luke 23:33-37

"When they had come to the place called Calvary, there they crucified him, and the criminals, one on the right hand and the other on the left. Then, Jesus said, "Father, forgive them, for they know not what they do."

And they divided his garments and cast lots. And the people stood looking on. But even the rulers with them sneered, saying, "He saved others; let him save himself if he is the Christ, the chosen of God."

The soldiers also mocked him, coming and offering him sour wine, and saying, "If you are the king of the Jews, save yourself."

Matthew 27:39-43

Those who passed by blasphemed him, wagging their heads and saying, "You who destroy the temple and build it in three days, save yourself! If you are the Son of God, come down from the cross." Likewise the chief priests also, mocking with the scribes and elders, said, "He saved others; himself he cannot save. If he is the king of Israel, let him now come down from the cross, and we will believe him. He trusted in God; let him deliver him now if he will have him; for he said, 'I am the Son of God.'"

Luke 23:39-43

Then, one of the criminals who were hanged hurled insults at him, saying, "If you are the Christ, save yourself and us."

But the other criminal rebuked him. "Don't you fear God," he said, "since you are under the same sentence? We are punished justly, for we are getting what our deeds deserve. But this man has done nothing wrong."

Then, he said to Jesus, "Lord, remember me when you come into your kingdom."

And Jesus said to him, "Assuredly, I say to you, today you will be with me in Paradise." NIV

THE GREAT CONTRAST

In the previous song for the SAVIOR Musical, I wanted the melody to reflect the taunting, prideful attitude surrounding Jesus on the cross. It is out of this dark manifestation of rebellious arrogance that the Lord prays here, "Father, forgive them, for they know not what they do." We tried our best to capture this contrast in the music itself. We wanted the listener to be swept from jagged hatred to the love and grace that enabled forgiveness. This is the center of the gospel.

THE POWER OF HIS FORGIVENESS

The studio was chaotic, noisy and exciting as the musicians prepared their parts for recording this song in Nashville. My wife, Britney, said, "Tell them what the song is about."

I held a talkback mic I used to sing a scratch vocal track, guiding them through the song. All I said to them through the mic, through the noise was, "Hey guys, just want to remind us all that this is the part where Jesus is on the cross." That was it. Then the studio went silent. Silence is a rarity in a recording studio, but it remained eerily quiet for a few long minutes... then we all felt something. At the risk of sounding super-spiritual, the best way to describe it is that the Spirit of the Lord felt almost tangible there in the studio. We were all in awe.

Overwhelmed, I started to cry, but they started to record. This presented a problem. Them recording meant I had to sing the scratch vocal... and it's pretty hard to sing while you're crying... but I couldn't stop. I'm not an easy crier, but there I was, surrounded by all of these pro musicians, sing-sobbing like a big baby. The take (they recorded) was beautiful and amazing, and, as far as I'm concerned, Spirit charged. You can hear it on the CD... minus the sing-sobbing vocal track. (For a hundred bucks, I'll let you hear it, though.)

THE THREE CROSSES OF CALVARY

There were three crosses on the hill of Calvary where Jesus was crucified. Christ's stood between two criminals'. We could call Jesus' *the cross of redemption*. The others we'll call *the cross of rejection* and *the cross of repentance*.

THE CROSS OF REJECTION

The criminal on the cross of rejection is at his end. He is in excruciating pain both physically and mentally. What is going on in his heart? He seems convinced that he's a victim in spite of the choices that brought him there. His life shouldn't end this way. He doesn't deserve this. He is boiling inside, and, out of his rage, unleashes a contemptuous tirade at Jesus, scoffing, "If you're the Christ..." This is not a question, but an accusation. Today this would sound something like, "If God were real, then why didn't he, why doesn't he... why didn't/does he allow... (add any presupposition here)." These accusations usually come down to God failing to create and maintain the world in keeping with the accuser's supreme wisdom; this is pride at its finest. *The cross of rejection* assumes no need of salvation or divine forgiveness. This criminal demands that Jesus prove himself by giving him what he wants; Jesus must solve his most immediate problems his way. Those "on this cross" reject Christ consciously when God fails to meet any number of personal expectations; they openly despise him. Those "on this cross" reject Christ unconsciously or inadvertently by their life choices, imagining themselves good enough to earn acceptance by God, wise enough to make their own way, rendering Jesus' sacrifice and God's Word superfluous to their life.

THE CROSS OF REPENTANCE

The criminal on *the cross of repentance* is at his end as well. He, too, is in excruciating pain both physically and mentally. What is going on in his heart? He knows he is getting his due. He deserves this fate. He accepts this as the consequence of his own life of choices. He rebukes the other criminal, challenging his lack of divine fear. Those who choose "this cross" do so from a recognition of who they are in relationship to God's holiness; they reverence him even in their sin. To them, God is just and their crimes justly punishable. This criminal entreats Jesus as Lord, hoping to be remembered, accepted, when Christ inherits his divine kingdom. Jesus welcomes him, "Today you will be with me in Paradise," requiring nothing else for his salvation. Faith demonstrated in repentance and confession is sufficient. By choosing *the cross of repentance*, we no longer live as a criminals, but as his forgiven sons, and daughters.

THE CROSS OF REDEMPTION

The whole world is represented on these two crosses. We choose, taking up either the *cross of rejection* or the *cross of repentance*. Standing in-between is *the cross of redemption*. Redemption basically means, getting back what's yours—it's a rescue. We are all criminals against God, but Christ took up "this cross" to save us from eternal punishment. Jesus said, "Greater love has no one than this, that someone lay down his life for his friends." Jesus takes this one step further on the *cross of redemption* by laying down his life for his enemies.

On the cross of redemption, Jesus prays, "Father, forgive them, for they know not what they do." He prays for his tormentors, but he also prays for our forgiveness.

The biblical term, forgiveness, is drawn from the financial world, expressing the relieving of debt. Here, it expresses God's mercy toward those who owe him an un-payable, eternal debt. Our debt is not financial, but moral and spiritual. It's beyond the scale of the debt owed to the parents of the boy we carelessly sped over while ignoring multiple warnings from school zone signs, flashing lights and screaming crossing guards. How could we even *begin* to repay such a debt. Just so, how could we hope to compensate for our contemptuous defilement of his holiness as we have both consciously and unconsciously broken his divine law.

It is for just such a group that Jesus prays. Nailed to the cross, Jesus pleads, "Father, forgive them, for they know not what they do." What spiritual ignorance we have of the eternal consequence of our sin. We don't know what we do, we don't know the awesomeness of his holiness and we don't know what our sin costs. If we did, we would understand the enormity of Jesus' sacrifice and of the love that compelled him to take up this *cross of redemption.*

Could there be a better picture of God's love and mercy? Ignorant man, nailing the Son of God to a cross as he cries out to the Father for their forgiveness. Our ignorance is no excuse for our sin, but Christ, here on the *cross of redemption,* extends an offer of forgiveness to us, to those who viciously and ignorantly put him on "that cross."

Understanding this is paramount. If we don't know the enormity of our offense against heaven, then our hearts shrink the enormity of the cross. If we don't understand the enormity of our sins, then our hearts shrink the enormity of his forgiveness. When we understand our atrocities against his holiness, then we are closer to understanding the vastness of his forgiveness, the enormity of his love and our role in the greatest love story ever told—God's rescue of fallen humanity through the willing Sacrifice of his Son, Jesus Christ, on a *cross of redemption.*

LIFE APPLICATIONS:

1. Have you ever been angry or disappointed with God. If so, why? Think of some conscious, or unconscious, ways you have rejected Christ in your life? What was the cause of this rejection?

_____

_____

_____

_____

_____

_____

_____

_____

_____

2. Think of a few times where you felt victimized even though you were fully or partially responsible for your situation. What are some ways that we shift blame away from ourselves in either our conscious or unconscious ways of rejecting Christ?

_____

_____

_____

_____

_____

_____

_____

_____

_____

3. Explain your thoughts about the role of personal responsibility in both the "cross of rejection" and the "cross of repentance." What are some things we can do to take more personal responsibility for our sinful choices?

_____

_____

_____

_____

_____

_____

_____

_____

_____

_____

4. How does Jesus' prayer, "Father forgive them, for they know not what they do," relate to your conscious and unconscious sins? How does understanding the enormity of your sins help you to better understand God's love and the enormity of his forgiveness?

_____

_____

_____

_____

_____

_____

_____

_____

33

MAY WE TAKE HIM DOWN?

John 19:28-37

Jesus, knowing all things were now accomplished, that the Scripture might be fulfilled, said, "I thirst!" Now a vessel full of sour wine was sitting there; and they filled a sponge with sour wine, put it on hyssop, and put it to his mouth. So when Jesus had received the sour wine, he said, "It is finished!" And bowing his head, he gave up his spirit.

Because it was Preparation Day, that the bodies should not remain on the cross on the Sabbath, the Jews asked Pilate that their legs might be broken that they might be taken away. Then, the soldiers came and broke the legs of the first and of the other who was crucified with him. But when they came to Jesus and saw that he was already dead, they did not break his legs. But one of the soldiers pierced his side with a spear, and immediately blood and water came out. And he who has seen has testified, and his testimony is true; and he knows that he is telling the truth, so that you may believe. For these things were done that the Scripture should be fulfilled, "Not one of his bones shall be broken." And again another Scripture says, "They shall look on him whom they pierced."

Matthew 27:45, 50-66

Now from the sixth hour until the ninth hour there was darkness over all the land. And Jesus cried out again with a loud voice, and yielded up his spirit. Then, behold, the veil of the temple was torn in two from top to bottom; and the earth quaked, and the rocks were split, and the graves were opened; and many bodies of the saints who had fallen asleep were raised; and coming out of the graves after his resurrection, they went into the holy city and appeared to many. So when the centurion and those with him, who were guarding Jesus, saw the earthquake and the things that had happened, they feared greatly, saying, "Truly this was the Son of God!"

And many women who followed Jesus from Galilee, ministering to him, were there looking on from afar, among whom were Mary Magdalene, Mary the mother of James and Joses, and the mother of Zebedee's sons.

When evening had come, there came a rich man from Arimathea, named Joseph, who himself had also become a disciple of Jesus. This man went to Pilate and asked for the body of Jesus. Then, Pilate commanded the body to be given to him. When Joseph had taken the body, he wrapped it in a clean linen cloth, and laid it in his new tomb which he had hewn out of the rock; and he rolled a large stone against the door of the tomb, and departed. And Mary Magdalene was there, and the other Mary, sitting opposite the tomb.

LAND OF SHADOWS

Here, Jesus dies on the cross and is laid in a cold, stone tomb. The disciples, his friends and family watched as he suffered on the cross, as he breathed his last, as he was buried. They were shocked, mortified. Their leader, their friend, one of their own was gone; laid dead in that tomb and with him—their hope.

Whatever glorious words poets may write on the subject of death, as if it is the final majestic experience of the caterpillar before becoming the butterfly, I think most would agree, if they're honest about what they know, as opposed to what they believe, that death is a fearful thing. We rarely want to talk about death these days. Why would we? It's the end of all we have known. As William Law writes, "When we consider death as a misery, we only think of it as a miserable separation from the enjoyments of this life."[ix] It can be a scary thing.

Scripture calls it a veil. (Isaiah 27) It's a devourer, (Job 18) strong and cruel, (Song 8) snaring men, (Psalm 18) seizing them with terror, (Psalm 55) swallowing them. (Psalm 49) It's like a net, snatching us unaware. (Ecclesiastes 9:12) The most common designation for death is as a land of darkness, a land of shadows, a place of no return. (Job 10) It is the common fate of all. (Psalm 89) We will each, in our own turn, die and face... Well, that's the point of calling it the land of shadows isn't it? We don't know what we will face. We have beliefs, but lack verifiable facts.

It is right to talk about death, however. For many ages of men, death was one of the most important things to consider. People spent their whole lives preparing to die, hoping for a good death. Our tendency, now, is to avoid the topic at all cost. Ecclesiastes 7:4-6 considers a contemplation of death a point of wisdom. At the risk of giving a cold and forensic answer to a profound soul laden question, however, I'll share with you some of my own experiences.

DEATH

I was first introduced to death when my grandmother's sister, Lena, died. I couldn't have been any older than three at the time. They held the viewing at her house. I remember not being allowed in the living room, because I was so young, but I could see her body lying in the casket from where I stood in the hall; my family and strangers were crying. I couldn't understand what was happening and had nightmares about it for years.

I grew up the youngest of three older brothers, Paul, Eric, Jason and an older sister, Kristen. Much of my childhood was spent at my grandparent's beautiful lake house in Massachusetts, swimming, boating, and playing—some of the best days of my life. My grandfather was a witty and kind, gentle man; he was a great painter. My grandmother was an artist, as well; she painted and played the piano, teaching me the basics of music on her spinet upright in the sunroom overlooking the lake.

My brother, Eric, had a knack for catching fish. The lake house had a long dock that stretched out over the water, and Eric would often fish with me at the end of that dock, showing me how to bait a hook, cast a line; he showed me where the bass hung out and how to reel'em in. He was a human fish-finder. I admired him so much growing up. I wanted to be like him. He was hilarious, a great teacher and listened to really cool music. As a kid, I would sit on his very tall bed up on our third floor, gazing at the art on his rock albums, as we listened to them. He'd tell me weird stories about the skeleton on one of his Grateful Dead T-shirts. He said it lived in the eaves of our house. When he wanted to get rid of me, he'd tell me that it would be coming out soon… so I'd better go downstairs. Throughout my life, he was careful not to make his youngest brother with the uneven bowl haircut feel unwelcome, or like the nuisance that I probably was.

I was four or five when my grandfather died. I didn't go to the funeral and I still had a hard time understanding what had happened. When I got the call a few years ago that my brother, Eric, had died suddenly, I was completely shocked. My head was scrambling to make sense of it. In my grieving, I wrote him a song that helped me to express my broken heart.

Eric had struggled with diabetes through his forties and had died unexpectedly in his sleep. He, my brother Jason and my mother were living in Florida; Britney and I were living in Nashville. Agreeing to perform my brother's funeral, I drove down to meet the rest of my family at Jason's, house, bringing a recording of Eric's song, "We'll Be Together." I hoped it would help everyone else cope, as well.

I could hear the crying as we walked up the driveway. It was comforting to be with my family… to grieve together. Being a Christian and in the ministry, I was asked the most pressing question on everyone's heart—"Why?" This was a spiritual question and it is the prevailing question in almost every human encounter with death. In those moments, when the reality of death comes crashing into our lives, our heart asks—"Why death?"

We want precise answers to this question. We want to console those who grieve with perfect words and explanations; we want to bring some perspective that will help. I know I did, but what could I say to my mom, to my brothers, to my sister, who had just lost a lifelong friend? What words would give consolation? What perspective could I give that would help? My brother was gone and nothing I could say or do would change that. I did my best, but nothing that I have ever done in the ministry was as spiritually and emotionally difficult as leading my own brother's funeral. I thought it would be appropriate here to present some of what I shared that day.

WHY DEATH?

The answer to the question, "Why death?" is important. There is something in all of us that says that death is wrong. We are spiritual beings with eternity in our hearts; we have everlasting souls. Though our bodies decay, grow sick, run down and die, Scripture tells us that we go on. Death conflicts with our eternity. Our spirits scream, "Not death! Life!"

God intended man to live forever, but, though shrouded in mystery, the Tree of Life teaches us that this immortality is the goal of creation and not its starting place. When Adam and Eve rebel, they are driven from paradise and from the Tree of Life within it. The reality of death enters the world as the result of their disobedience, and from Adam to us, sin has reigned and death is its greatest accomplishment. The Apostle Paul says, "Therefore, just as sin came into the world through one man, and death through sin, and so death spread to all men because all sinned." (Romans 5:12) This body, this earth suit that we all live in, has to die before eternity, because it is corrupted, diseased, as it were, by sin.

In addition to our physical death, however, we can see three other types of death that occur as a result of sin. Moral death destroys our nature. Spiritual death destroys our capacity to commune with God. Eternal death is, as the name suggests, final death... the condemnation of an eternal soul to everlasting separation from the presence of God.

IT IS FINISHED

For us, as for the disciples, the confrontation with death is a trying time for the soul. Even Jesus wept when Lazarus died, knowing full well that he would raise him up. Jesus relates with us in our grief; it breaks his heart that we endure such sorrow.

When Jesus breathes his last on the cross, he says, "It is finished." He has accomplished something, but, at this point, his words are lost on his disciples. Jesus' death is their only present reality. What they don't know is that, in the death of Jesus is the death of death.

LIFE APPLICATIONS:

1. Do you tend to distract yourself from thinking about death? Explain.

_____

_____

_____

_____

_____

_____

_____

_____

_____

_____

2. Do you imagine that contemplating your inevitable death, or the deaths of your loved ones, would make your life more miserable or more meaningful? Explain.

_____

_____

_____

_____

_____

_____

_____

_____

_____

3. If you knew that you had one more year to live, how would you live differently? What would you change? How do you suppose this would affect your perspective on life?

_____

_____

_____

_____

_____

_____

_____

_____

_____

_____

4. How do your beliefs about God affect your ability to cope with other people's and your own eventual death?

_____

_____

_____

_____

_____

_____

_____

_____

_____

34

ADONAI

Psalm 35:22

This you have seen, O Lord; Do not keep silence. O LORD, be not far from me.

Psalm 38:9;21-22

LORD, all my desire is before you; and my sighing is not hidden from you. Do not forsake me, O Lord; O my God, be not far from me! Make haste to help me, O LORD, my salvation!

Psalm 77:1-12

I cried out to God for help; I cried out to God to hear me. When I was in distress, I sought the LORD; at night I stretched out untiring hands and my soul refused to be comforted. I remembered you, O God, and I groaned; I mused, and my spirit grew faint.

You kept my eyes from closing; I was too troubled to speak. I thought about the former days, the years of long ago; I remembered my songs in the night. My heart mused and my spirit inquired:

"Will the LORD reject forever? Will he never show his favor again? Has his unfailing love vanished forever? Has his promise failed for all time? Has God forgotten to be merciful? Has he in anger withheld his compassion?"

Then, I thought, "To this I will appeal: the years of the right hand of the Most High." I will remember the deeds of the Lord; yes, I will remember your miracles of long ago. I will meditate on all your works and consider all your mighty deeds. NIV

FAR FROM GOD

"He's dead, Brian." My words hung over us like a leaden cloud as Brian, the drummer in our band, The Trees, gazed in confused duress trying to identify the victim. The headlights from the passing cars shone on the young boy's body motionless on the side of the highway. A look of horror swept over his face, as he escalated from a flat murmur to a fevered pitch, "No, that's Scott; that's Scott!" on and on again. Brian told me later that he knew him by his sneakers. They'd been close friends since childhood; Scott was only 17.

We were heading down I95 on our way back from a Steve Miller concert in my 66' Chevelle when we came across the SUV, upturned aside the Jersey Barrier, wheels still spinning, people crawling from its shattered windows. Brian recognized his friend's car, so we pulled over. Beer cans had spilled from the wreck and lay strewn across the highway; we were with them earlier, all coming from the same concert. There weren't any emergency personnel on the scene yet, so I checked on the kid face down a few feet in front of the car. I knelt and placed two fingers behind his ear, feeling for a pulse... nothing. "C'mon kid..." I muttered, anxious for any sign of life.

His friends were wailing in the background; the driver of the car kept his distance and kept yelling, "This isn't happening... this isn't happening!" But it was happening. It was happening before our eyes.

Soon, an ambulance arrived, and the paramedics rushed the poor kid to the hospital. We followed and waited outside, hoping the doctors were able to bring him back, but the boy's parents came out, crying. His father pleaded with us as he lead his sobbing wife through the waiting room, "Just learn something from this, just learn something..." I was learning something alright; I didn't know him, but it was a lesson that would dramatically change my life.

They held Scott's funeral at an old white New England church. I stood in the parking lot outside, listening with the sun warm on my face to the eulogy being broadcast to the overflow crowd. The Priest said, "Scott experienced God in the mountaintops while he hiked, Scott experienced God in the waves as he surfed," and so on. He was a good kid, I thought, knowing that I wasn't. I asked myself, *When do I experience God?* I didn't, and I really didn't like myself that day. If anyone spoke such kind words at my funeral, they'd be lying. I needed to change; I wanted to change; I wanted to experience God.

LORD

The title of this song is just one word—*Adonai*... a Hebrew word meaning Lord, or Master. It is the form of this word "Lord" that is used in the supplicating Psalms above. The psalmist, sensing the distance between him and God, pleads, "Adonai, be not far from me?"

This song is a musical recognition of the Sabbath after Jesus' death, a silent period in the gospel story that should not be overlooked emotionally. The gospels themselves leave this day unexplored, but it is rewarding to give that day its gloomy due. These Psalms and this song capture the despair, confusion, disappointment and fear I believe stormed inside the hearts of the disciples during these prolonged hours. When our faith is tried, we can feel distant, alone, scared, even forsaken by God.

WHERE AM I?

We all walk through dark times in life, times when we feel distant from God. I've felt it; I'm sure you've felt it and Jesus' disciples felt it on that dismal Sabbath day. Sometimes it's easy to forget that these disciples were people just like you and I, but if we put ourselves in their shoes, (or sandals) we'd see that they had all the feelings that come with being human. They were men and women who put their faith in Jesus as their Messiah and everyday for three years, they walked with Christ, listened to his teachings, followed his lead, watched him perform many miracles... but then he was gone... and gone with him was every dream and hope that had fed their imaginations and, yes, their faith. They were devout servants of

Christ, but this Sabbath day was a dark night for their souls. Though God was near, and a glorious dawn was coming, their hearts knew nothing of it.

KNOWN & UNKNOWN

A powerful emotional contrast develops in Jesus' arrest and crucifixion between Jesus' perception of these events and the disciples' perception of them. Jesus, who knew the will and plan of the Father, walked willingly into this entire affair. He suffered a death as horrific as one might only imagine in nightmares, but breathed his last with the words, "It is finished," on his pummeled lips. Jesus has just completed the work of the ages. He had reversed the curse against the children of Adam, opening a path to God for all who would truly believe. He knew the proper implications of millennia of prophecies regarding his work. He knew who he was, where he was going, and what was coming next.

The disciples, on this silent Sabbath day, know none of this. Like the arc of the earth to the human eye, the arc of God's plan is too large for their souls to make out... they don't see beyond their present darkness. With Jesus' arrest and death, they have entered into what one saint has called "The Dark Night of the Soul." The disciples knew the Scriptures, they believed Jesus to be the Christ, but their vision of what that meant in the larger scheme of things was so skewed as to leave them blind-sided now. Jesus, crucified, dead and lying in a stone tomb was not part of their hopes and dreams and they were confused by all of Jesus' attempts to prepare them for these very events. What they have now, standing in the shadow of the cross, on that dark Sabbath are broken hearts, dashed dreams, failed hopes, increasing despair, and rising threat against their very lives for their open association with a crucified insurrectionist. Where was God in any of this?

GOD IS NOT FAR

We are primarily motivated by the incentives of gain and are shaped by our experiences. When we have expended ourselves to no profit, whether financial, emotional, or spiritual we can lose heart and lose the drive to continue sacrificing. Disappointments in life can greatly affect a person's faith. It is hard to be full of faith when disappointments, confusion, and/or physical, emotional, or social disasters have drained us. So where do we go to refill? Where do we go for our encouragement in these dark hours of the soul? Trite answers, no matter how well meaning, are rarely helpful, and I hope this won't seem like one of them... but... when suffering through a sense of separation from God, we must remember that God loves us. God is good. God is all knowing and all wise. God has a plan. We're a part of it. God's plan is too big and too complex for us to perceive most of it, but he's given many promises in guidance and many promises in his Word. We're called to trust him. He will bring us through "The Dark Night of the Soul" if we cling in faith to him. Cry out to him like the psalmists in your anguish, but settle your heart on his love for you. Even if you imagine that you will never be happy again, know that God is not as far from you as you may think.

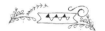

LIFE APPLICATIONS:

1. How have disappointments in your life affected your faith? Give some examples.

   _____

   _____

   _____

   _____

   _____

   _____

   _____

   _____

   _____

   _____

2. Think about some of the darkest moments in your life. What was it that caused you to feel either distant from God's love, plan or wisdom or near to them? If you've experienced both reactions, talk a little about the differences between them.

   _____

   _____

   _____

   _____

   _____

   _____

   _____

   _____

   _____

   _____

3. Was there a time in your life when you were stronger in faith than you are today? If so, what fueled your faith? What do you suppose would help you recover it?

_____

_____

_____

_____

_____

_____

_____

4. Do you feel distant from God now? How have you been experiencing God lately?

_____

_____

_____

_____

_____

_____

_____

35

THE LIVING AMONG THE DEAD

Mark 16:1-4

And when the Sabbath was past, Mary Magdalene, and Mary the mother of James, and Salome, had bought sweet spices, that they might come and anoint him. And very early in the morning the first day of the week, they came unto the sepulcher at the rising of the sun.

And they said among themselves, "Who shall roll the stone away from the door of the tomb for us?" And when they looked, they saw that the stone was rolled away: for it was very large.

Luke 24:4-5

And it happened, as they were greatly perplexed about this, that behold, two men stood by them in shining garments. Then, as they were afraid and bowed their faces to the earth, they said to them, "Why do you seek the living among the dead?"

Matthew 28:5-7

"Do not be afraid, for I know that you seek Jesus who was crucified. He is not here; for he is risen, as he said. 'The Son of Man must be delivered into the hands of sinful men, and be crucified, and the third day rise again.' And they remembered his words. (Luke 24:7-8) Come; see the place where the Lord lay. And go quickly and tell his disciples that he is risen from the dead, and, indeed, he is going before you into Galilee; there you will see him. Behold, I have told you."

Mark 16:8

So they went out quickly and fled from the tomb, for they trembled and were amazed. And they said nothing to anyone, for they were afraid.

AT THE RISING OF THE SUN

It is still dark when these women set out early for the tomb. Their hearts are burdened with two days of mourning as they trudge through the darkness, carrying spices to anoint the corpse of their dead lord. Could this day start off any gloomier? Dawn is not yet upon them. The birds are silent; the world is yet asleep; the chill of early morning is blanketed with an eerie stillness, save for the shuffling of their sandals on the gravel roads and their hushed whispers... "Who will roll away the stone?"

They mourn not only a beloved teacher but also the death of their hopes and dreams. Jesus has dominated years of their life, lifting them out of the drudgery of mere survival into the glory of living with divine purpose. He is gone and meaning lies dead in the tomb with him. They have had two days to set their minds to a new course, no... an old course... a life without Jesus and without any greater goal than simply living on. Before he came, they had little, but they had contentment; they'd accustomed themselves to life's monotony. Now, however, having witnessed his miracles, wondered at his teaching, been moved by his promises, even the hope of contentment is gone. In the end, they exchanged satisfaction for short-lived thrills, ruining life as they knew it.

The thin light of dawn is breaking now as they reach the stone tomb. Through the mist, they notice something's wrong. Very wrong. When they last saw the tomb, a huge rock was rolled over the entrance, guards were stationed there to protect the body from being stolen. Now the stone that had worried their minds as they walked was rolled away; the tomb was opened. *Who could have done this?* Confusion and fear sets in as they grapple for answers.

EXPECTATION

These women had expectations. Expectation is a powerful force. When we are set to confront an anticipated reality, change or difference can throw us into turmoil... even small adjustments... even when a situations proves better than expected. Some experiences can be so radical as to completely unhinge our worldview. Our perceptions of reality can crash and even the most foundational beliefs can fall under suspicion when our expectations are not met. Whether this trauma is good or bad in the end, the process itself can be saturated with frightening possibilities.

I remember when my worldview started to become a little unhinged. I was driving by the church down the street from me, where a year later, I would attend and commit my life to Christ. As I drove by, I felt something eerily strange—the thought of God entered my mind. I had a vague belief in God at the time, but imagined him to be about as connected and attentive to my life as jolly ole' Saint Nick, in spite of my childhood experience with him (Jesus, not Santa). As my car passed the church, it was as if it passed through a sudden fog, as if I'd driven into an idea—*what-if God isn't as distant as I expected*. It was more than a thought, because for a brief moment, I suspended all I held to be true of God. I caught an impression of an immanent God, a present and caring God. I was challenged and frightened by the idea and quickly tried my best to disregard it. If it were true, then I was not ready to accept, or deal its implications. The door that kept God out of my life was becoming unhinged and I didn't like it. It scared me. I didn't know what to do about it. I most likely turned up the music and kept driving. I learned later of that church's new pastor and his custom of going into the sanctuary to pray for the community. Perhaps I drove into one of his prayers.

ANGELS AMONG US

As they enter Jesus' tomb, they discover that Jesus' body is gone. Here begins a pained dance with confusion. Each of the gospels unpack various aspects of what was a chaotic morning for these women. Disoriented by a moved stone and a missing body, his clothes the only memorial left to him, they are on the brink of a face to face confrontation with supernatural forces—they're not alone in that tomb.

Sacred story comes to life as angels appear in glowing robes, striking fear in their hearts, driving them trembling, faces to the ground before them. The angels' words are unsettling. "Why do you seek the living among the dead?" Jesus, they say, has risen, just as he told them many times he would. *Hmmmm… always thought that was some kind of metaphor.* The angels commission them. The women are to go to the disciples and tell them that when Jesus said he would be killed and rise again, he meant he would be killed and rise again… not in some distant resurrection at the end of time, but now. Jesus will meet them in Galilee. They flee, trembling, amazed, terrified, and full of confused joy at the very idea that Jesus could be alive. The possibility of what they thought they'd lost was, perhaps, even greater than they suspected.

CONFLICTED

When the supernatural breaks into the natural, we begin to question what is natural. When divine truth first begins to press itself destructively against the many fallacies crafted elegantly to excuse human corruption, when it forces its foot into the closing door of our secularism, when it breaks like the dawn into our darkness, it threatens treasured reality; it overturns our sense of control and stability. It both repels us in fear of the unknown and draws us in fascination with the possibilities. Like these women who ran from the tomb, we can be scared, but excited, overwhelmed, but overjoyed, confused, but on the edge of enlightenment. Everything hinges on what we do next. When the supernatural breaks into our natural world, there is a reaction, a suspension of reality, but then, there's a response. The truth of God is terrifying; it makes unprecedented demands on our lives. We can rationalize it away and go back to life as usual, or we can launch ourselves into the adventure of a lifetime.

LIFE APPLICATIONS:

1. Describe in your own words what kind of spiritual encounter this devotional is talking about.

_____

_____

_____

_____

_____

_____

_____

_____

2. Have you ever experienced this kind of life-altering "conflicted encounter" with God or Scripture? If so, describe the difference between your emotional reaction in the moment and your ultimate response to the event.

_____

_____

_____

_____

_____

_____

_____

_____

_____

3. Has there been a time when your beliefs, your perception of reality, and/or your worldview was threatened? If so, how did it affect your life? Give details. Describe the difference between your emotional reaction in the moment and your ultimate response to the event.

_____

_____

_____

_____

_____

_____

_____

_____

_____

_____

36

WOMAN

John 20:1-1

Now the first day of the week Mary Magdalene went to the tomb early, while it was still dark, and saw that the stone had been taken away from the tomb. Then, she ran and came to Simon Peter, and to the other disciple, whom Jesus loved, and said to them, "They have taken away the Lord out of the tomb, and we do not know where they have laid him."

Peter therefore went out, and the other disciple, and were going to the tomb. So they both ran together, and the other disciple outran Peter and came to the tomb first. And he, stooping down and looking in, saw the linen cloths lying there; yet he did not go in. Then, Simon Peter came, following him, and went into the tomb; and he saw the linen cloths lying there, and the handkerchief that had been around his head, not lying with the linen cloths, but folded together in a place by itself. Then, the other disciple, who came to the tomb first, went in also; and he saw and believed. For as yet they did not know the Scripture, that he must rise again from the dead. Then, the disciples went away again to their own homes.

But Mary stood outside by the tomb crying, and as she wept she stooped down and looked into the tomb. And she saw two angels in white sitting, one at the head and the other at the feet, where the body of Jesus had lain. Then, they said to her, "Woman, why are you crying?"

She said to them, "Because they have taken away my Lord, and I do not know where they have laid him."

Now when she had said this, she turned around and saw Jesus standing there, and did not know that it was Jesus. Jesus said to her, "Woman, why are you crying? Who are you looking for?"

She, supposing him to be the gardener, said to him, "Sir, if you have carried him away, tell me where you have laid him, and I will take him away."

Jesus said to her, "Mary!"

She turned and said to him, "Rabboni!" (which is to say, Master).

Jesus said to her, "Do not cling to me, for I have not yet ascended to my Father; but go to my brethren and tell them, 'I am ascending to my Father and your Father, and to my God and your God.'"

MARY MAGDALENE

Every Easter when I was a child, my father would watch the Jesus of Nazareth movie. The scene at the tomb never failed to dazzle my curiosity; it was so vividly supernatural to me—Supposed gardeners asking alluring questions of confused women reeling from the shock of an empty tomb, time itself freezing like the early morning air around them to frame the moment when the supernatural breaks into the natural.

It can be hard to disentangle the exact procession of events involving the women who went that fateful Sunday morning to anoint the dead body of Jesus—together, then separating, coming and going as the morning progresses; they discover his absence, encounter angels, engage the disbelieving disciples. Though these accounts could be harmonized, John takes a special interest in Mary Magdalene (Magdalene being her place of origin, not her last name). Mark says that Jesus appears first to her, from whom he had cast out seven demonic spirits. (Mark 16:9) She appears to struggle the most with the angelic announcements, unable to comprehend it all. While some appear from other gospel accounts to realize the identity of these angelic figures, taking joy at their announcement, fearful as they were at the idea of Jesus' resurrection, Mary cannot get her head around it.

This was a dark time for Mary. She stood outside that stone cold tomb of lost hope, crying, overcome with disappointment, confusion and sadness at the death of Jesus, like all the others. She, however, had been delivered by him from more dire circumstances than they. The loss of Jesus, their master, might send the others back to the humdrum existence of mere survival, but she had been a demonized woman of ill repute. He had not only cast out those demons, but had defended her before the local authorities, tolerating and even praising her outrageous displays of repentance and desperation, (Luke 7:36-39) and had defended her again before her scolding sister, permitting her to sit at his feet while he taught her, along with the twelve. He had raised her brother from the grave. Now, *Jesus* is dead, and no amount of promises to the contrary from resplendent figures in white can break through her disbelieving depression.

DEPRESSION

What Mary sensed in these sad moments, many people live with. People live day to day with either an underlying, or an overwhelming sense of sadness and can live in this constant state of depression throughout all of their lives. Depression is a real and tragic problem of epidemic proportions.

Before I came to Christ, I struggled with depression. I tried to self-medicate and self-soothe, but it did nothing to fix the problem. I had coping mechanisms: I would party to try and raise my spirits, but that was a short-lived fix. Depression closed in quickly again. I would try to stay sober, but that didn't abate the sadness and anxiety. I would lose myself in my music, but sometimes that made it worse. A good song written in those moments had a way of encapsulating, almost enshrining, the depression, dredging up the feeling with every recital. I tried to find meaning in relationships, but still nothing. It seemed there wasn't anything I could do to find a cure, to keep that slow undercurrent of sadness from dragging me down on a daily basis. I didn't understand where the sadness came from and tried to resign myself to living out my days under its spell.

Even heavier states of depression would come in waves. In these times, I would lock myself away for days, not wanting to see or talk with anybody. The whole world seemed filled with woe; I felt like I could cry at the opening of a supermarket.[x] I was driven person, however, driven to be a great songwriter, have a great band, do great things, but this caused me a great amount of anxiety and I worried constantly… my friends worried, too. I wouldn't return their phone calls, and resisted hanging out. They could tell something was wrong, but I had no good answer for their pressing questions. When I came to Christ, I felt like he asked me the same type of question, he asked Mary, "Why are you so sad?"

MASTER

Leaving two angelic hosts behind, Mary turns from the tomb and encounters Jesus himself. She cannot see through her gloom to recognize him, however.[xi] She takes him for a gardener and inquires after the body of her master… standing alive, mere feet in front of her. Then, Jesus speaks her name. "Mary!" he says.

Is there any word in a person's vocabulary more compelling than his or her own name? Even animals come to recognize it, hearing when we speak, "blah, blah, blah, blah, Roadie, blah blah blah."[xii] That word can penetrate the most cacophonous event, traveling distinct through a myriad of voices into our senses. Our names represent us, the first of all words that we seem to respond to as babies. Names are typically the first offering in relationship building. Those who know us best often choose special names for us, based not on parental forethought, but relational afterthought, being truer to nature, reminiscent of a known past… or, in the cases of God and Jesus, of a known future; Abram becomes Abraham and Simon becomes Peter (Rock).

God knows us intimately and comforts us, he calls out to us, saying, "Fear not, for I have redeemed you; I have called you by name, you are mine." (Isaiah 43:1) The Servant of the LORD boasts of such intimacies, saying, "The LORD called me from the womb, from the body of my mother he named my name." (Isaiah 49:1) Jesus, the Good Shepherd, "calls his own sheep by name and leads them out. ...the sheep follow him, for they know his voice." (John 10:3-4)

Jesus proves it now. With that singularly personal word, "Mary!" Jesus penetrates her darkness, sweeps away her doubt, lifts her depression. Her blind eyes are opened and she knows him for who and what he is. "Master!" she cries.

HE CALLED MY NAME

The day I sat in that small New England church for the first time, I heard the Lord "call *my* name." It was like the dawn breaking into my darkness. *He knows me!* He knew me and knew where I was, what I was dealing with, the sadness and anxiety I was living with and He knows you. He knows us all by name, he knows us intimately, even down to the very number of hairs on our heads. When he calls us we know that he isn't a distant character, a mere role model in an ancient book; he's alive, close. He knows you, knows your disappointments, knows your hurts, your issues, your circumstances in life, your anxiety, your sadness, your fears, your sins. He knows you, loves you and desires a relationship with you. When he calls you, listen. He is able to turn your sorrow into joy, give meaning to your existence, comfort you in your pain and give boldness in your fear. He has overcome sin, hell and death for you, so that you no longer have to walk in the darkness; but you can be with him, walk with him, and live in the light and overwhelming joy of life.

Here are some practical steps you can take to put yourself in the way of divine encounter. 1. Set aside time each day to read Scripture in an environment conducive to meditating on God. 2. Pray each day not just about your needs, but in meditation on God and in gratitude for the things he done for you generally and specifically. 3. Take advantage of times of worship both corporate and private... singing helps. 4. Pray that God will reveal himself to you and be ready to embrace it.

LIFE APPLICATIONS:

1. Have you ever lived with an underlying, or overwhelming sense of sadness or depression? If yes, what were, or are, some of your coping mechanisms? i.e. self-medicating and self-soothing? Do you have a sense of what caused, or causes, your sadness?

_____

_____

_____

_____

_____

_____

_____

_____

_____

_____

2. Give your own definition of joy. How have you known joy in your life? Do you believe that Jesus is a legitimate source of joy in this world?

_____

_____

_____

_____

_____

_____

_____

_____

_____

3. Have you ever experienced the risen Christ? Have you ever heard him "call your name?" Describe the experience. What were the after effects?

_____

_____

_____

_____

_____

_____

_____

_____

_____

_____

37

I'VE SEEN HIM

Matthew 28:8-10

So the women went out quickly from the tomb with fear and great joy, and ran to bring his disciples word. And as they went to tell his disciples, behold, Jesus met them, saying, "Rejoice!" So they came and held him by the feet and worshiped him. Then, Jesus said to them, "Do not be afraid. Go and tell my brethren to go to Galilee, and there they will see me."

Luke 24:8-15

And they remembered his words. Then, they returned from the tomb and told all these things to the eleven and to all the rest. It was Mary Magdalene, Joanna, Mary the mother of James, and the other women with them, who told these things to the apostles. And their words seemed to them like idle tales, and they did not believe them. But Peter arose and ran to the tomb; and stooping down, he saw the linen cloths lying by themselves; and he departed, marveling to himself at what had happened.

John 20:18

Mary Magdalene came and told the disciples that she had seen the Lord, and that he had spoken these things to her.

Mark 16:9-13

Now when he rose early on the first day of the week, he appeared first to Mary Magdalene, out of whom he had cast seven demons. She went and told those who had been with him, as they mourned and wept. And when they heard that he was alive and had been seen by her, they did not believe.

FEAR AND GREAT JOY

Jesus could have revealed himself first to Peter if he chose to. He could have sent his angels to anyone he wanted. He decided, for his own purposes, to reveal himself to these women, coming in the early pre-dawn darkness, wallowing in their sorrow and disappointed hopes, to attend to his corpse. The process of this experience is enlightening. In chapter 35, we focused on the women's confusion, that bewildered wonderment at the angelic announcement of Jesus' resurrection, and how it unseated their hold on a reality without Christ, their begrudging return to life as usual. In chapter 36, we focused with John on Mary Magdalene, who, being the most resistant to these angelic announcements is pulled from her depression and incredulity by a face to face encounter with the risen Christ, who calls her name. Here, in this chapter, we want to turn our attention to the third part of the event as commonly presented. The risen Christ reveals himself first to Mary and then to the other women, banishing sorrow, disappointment, depression and hopelessness. Then, he commissions them. These women become his witnesses to his closest disciples. "Go," he says, "and tell my brethren to go to Galilee, and there they will see me."

Interestingly enough, the disciples do not believe the women at first. Mark 16:11 is rather plain about it, saying, "But when they heard that he was alive and had been seen by her, they would not believe it." Luke 24:10-11 is a bit more detailed, "Now it was Mary Magdalene, Joanna, Mary, the mother of James, and the other women with them who told these things to the apostles, but these words seemed to them an idle tale, and they did not believe them."

Something, however, caused Peter to doubt his own doubt, to go and see. I can only imagine that it was the changed lives of these women. They went out mourning, but returned rejoicing, went out full of sorrow, but returned beaming with elation. The disciples must have wondered what could have befallen them to bring about such a change, to strip away that mountain of grief. They'd soon find out. John tells of Peter's attempt to see for himself, going to the tomb, and of his own disbelief of the women's testimony, until he saw Jesus' empty grave clothes. (John 20:3-10) The word that they initially rebuffed had finally found its home in the hearts of some of the eleven, and they go, as instructed by Jesus through the women, to the place of his choosing, hoping to see him there.

BUT NOW I SEE

Much like these women, when I first experienced the risen Christ in my own life, I ran and told many close friends and family. I could hardly keep it to myself. Also, like these women, however, I was met by doubt and unbelief. Some of my friends told me I'd been brainwashed, or that I'd conjured it all up in my imagination; others just told me to keep it to myself and that I shouldn't go around preaching to everyone… but how could I not? I was changed by the supernatural power of Christ; Jesus was real and alive in my life and he wanted me to go and tell. It was like the lyrics in the song Amazing Grace, "I was blind, but now I see." I didn't realize that I was blind, until I'd seen the Lord, and, having seen him, I wanted all of my friends and all of my family to see him too. If I'd found the cure for blindness. How selfish would I have to be to keep it to myself?

I don't intend to diminish the noble work of those who dedicate their lives to apologetics, establishing defenses of Scripture, or of the claims of God and Christ in them, but anyone who wishes to remain somewhat sane as a witness for Christ must realize that it is our duty to go and tell, not to argue and convince. We want to be clear preachers, good witnesses, reasonable arguers, loving Christians, but, in the end, it is always the revelation of the resurrected Christ to a person's own heart that convinces. The power of our own joy and the witness of our own changed life can be a powerful tools in telling people about the realities of Jesus Christ, but, in the end, without the conviction of the Holy Spirit and a genuine encounter with God in Christ, the best we can hope for is convincing people that they should find better community, or strive to live more moral lives. Transformation of the soul before a God seeking true disciples requires a confrontation with a new reality found in a resurrected SAVIOR.

LIFE APPLICATIONS:

1. Have *you* ever rejected someone who shared Christ with you? Like the disciples, did their testimony sound like "idle tales"?

_____

_____

_____

_____

_____

_____

_____

_____

_____

_____

2. Have you ever been rejected for sharing Christ? How did you deal with it? Did you feel a personal responsibility to convince them? Talk about it.

_____

_____

_____

_____

_____

_____

_____

_____

_____

3. If you have ever felt exuberant and joyful about Christ, did that exuberance cause you to tell many people about your experience? Think of some examples. Has your desire to share Christ with others waned over time?

_____

_____

_____

_____

_____

_____

_____

_____

_____

4. It is natural for exuberance over anything to wax and wane repeatedly over time. What could you do to keep your exuberance for sharing Christ alive in your life?

_____

_____

_____

_____

_____

_____

_____

_____

38

PEACE BE WITH YOU

Luke 24:36-39

While they were still talking about this, Jesus himself stood among them and said to them, "Peace be with you."

They were startled and frightened, thinking they saw a ghost. He said to them, "Why are you troubled, and why do doubts rise in your minds? Look at my hands and my feet. It is I myself! Touch me and see; a ghost does not have flesh and bones, as you see I have." NIV

John 20:19-30

On the evening of that first day of the week, when the disciples were together, with the doors locked for fear of the Jewish leaders, Jesus came and stood among them and said, "Peace be with you!" After he said this, he showed them his hands and side. The disciples were overjoyed when they saw the Lord.

Again Jesus said, "Peace be with you! As the Father has sent me, I am sending you." And with that he breathed on them and said, "Receive the Holy Spirit. If you forgive anyone's sins, their sins are forgiven; if you do not forgive them, they are not forgiven."

Now Thomas (also known as Didymus), one of the Twelve, was not with the disciples when Jesus came. So the other disciples told him, "We have seen the Lord!"

But he said to them, "Unless I see the nail marks in his hands and put my finger where the nails were, and put my hand into his side, I will not believe."

A week later his disciples were in the house again, and Thomas was with them. Though the doors were locked, Jesus came and stood among them and said, "Peace be with you!" Then, he said to Thomas, "Put your finger here; see my hands. Reach out your hand and put it into my side. Stop doubting and believe."

Thomas said to him, "My Lord and my God!"

Then, Jesus told him, "Because you have seen me, you have believed; blessed are those who have not seen and yet have believed."

Jesus performed many other signs in the presence of his disciples, which are not recorded in this book. NIV

PEACE

You never forget a first impression. My first impression of Jesus was his peace. I told the story in chapter 27 of an encounter I had with the Spirit of Christ when I was in the 4th grade. I was going through a custody battle and had been sent from my father's house to live with my mother. She enrolled me in a new school, and, the night after my first day of school, I awoke in great fear, convulsing. The teacher taught us the 1st day that if we were ever afraid just to say, "Jesus, be with me now." Not knowing much of the Bible, or of Jesus, other than that he was God, I began repeating. "Jesus, be with me now… Jesus be with me now." Suddenly, he *was* with me. I sensed his presence in the room in an almost tangible way; it calmed my fears and brought a powerful sense of peace. I had never encountered real peace until then.

RESSURECTION

After Jesus' resurrection, his first words to the gathered disciples, as he enters into their midst, are "Peace, be with you." He says it twice. Jesus' popping into their midst as they cowered inside a locked room, certainly, wouldn't have added to their calm; they are horrified and shriek as if seeing a ghost. (Luke 24:37) Their distress goes far beyond that, however. Indeed, there had been little peace in their lives since that horrible night of his arrest outside Gethsemane, as they fled, followed at a distance, denied him, wept bitterly, heard of his condemnation, beating and crucifixion and hid in fear of "the Jews." Like the women, their messianic hopes had been set upon Jesus, and they too were crushed, dispirited and depressed. To make matters worse, they have been plagued since early morning by uncertainty in the wake of the women's testimony of the empty tomb (they'd seen that for themselves) and that angelic hosts had declared him risen, (hysterical women, perhaps) and that the women had even claimed to see Jesus alive and kicking thereafter (hallucinations, no doubt). No... peace is the last thing these disciples have, but it's the first thing Jesus offers them.

Here begins an important exchange with the disciples. Jesus goes out of his way to convince them that he is not a spirit, but is flesh and blood, a living human being. He encourages them to look him over, to touch him; he eats in front of them. Then, Jesus begins to unpack the import of his resurrection from the Scriptures. Indeed, this encounter with the risen Christ is the most radically transforming event of their lives, converting them, here and now, from men hiding from authorities, shattered in their personal hopes in Jesus, into fearless champions for the Kingdom of God... fishermen ready to take on the world. Indeed, the resurrection of Jesus is the most significant event in the New Testament. It transformed a local Jewish rabbi, murdered by jealous competitors, into the most famous and influential figure in human history, making the resurrection the most significant *event* in world history as well.

Resurrection is not just one more miracle tossed on top of a healthy career of amazing miracles. It is the miracle of all miracles; its implications are staggering to the mind. Jesus is the first and only person, thus far, to be resurrected from the dead. The Apostle Paul says Jesus is, "the firstborn from the dead," (Colossians 1:18) and "the first fruits of those who have fallen asleep." (I Corinthians 15:20) True resurrection is not just resuscitation. A few people have been resuscitated in the Bible: the two dead boys with Elijah and Elisha, (1 Kings 17; 2 Kings 4) the dead man who lands on the bones of Elisha, (2 Kings 13:20ff) Lazarus, of course, (Luke 11) the little 12 year old daughter of Jairus (Mark 5) and, even, the youth from the funeral at Nain. (Luke 7) These were raised from the dead their same old selves, destined to die again in time. Jesus, however, as is evidenced by his actions since his resurrection (disappearing, appearing, walking through walls when it suits him, later, taking off like a rocket into the clouds) has taken on immortal flesh, taking up residence in both the physical and spiritual realm at one and the same time. He is the embodiment of Jewish hopes for a new earth, incorruptible, not subject to death, able to stand unharmed before an unveiled holy God. Paul echoes this description, "How are the dead raised? With what kind of body do they come? …What is sown is perishable; what is raised is imperishable. It is sown in dishonor; it is raised in glory. It is sown in weakness; it is raised in power. It is sown a natural body; it is raised a spiritual body. (1 Corinthians 15:35, 42-44) These disciples are transformed when they realize that every promise of the prophets is standing unquestionably before them. It's ALL true. They know it by more than blind faith... for its surety is speaking with them.

This resurrection means more. It means that Jesus, as a new Adam, has become the corporate head of a new humanity. As Noah's righteousness permitted not only his own salvation from the flood, but, also, that of his wife, daughters'-in-law, and sons—even Ham. So too, Jesus' righteousness covers all those believing in him, those who abide "in him," bringing them safely through the fiery judgment that is divine holiness. As their corporate head, he offers himself on behalf of the whole as a willing sacrifice to atone for their sin, passing into the ordeal of death... and, being found acceptable, chosen by God, is raised from the dead in the fullness of the resurrection life that was promised of old to all who are found acceptable before God. Every promise is made true in him.

This is their peace. Peace with God. Peace in their souls, knowing that they have nothing to fear... not even death. Jesus has gone through that veil, entered into that dark realm, cast light for them over that land of shadows, has returned from the place of no return and has declared peace to them. All is well. All will be well. Nothing can harm them, not even death itself. He's been there, done that, and they have nothing in this world to fear.

Jesus promised those who believe in him, "Peace I leave with you; my peace I give you. I do not give to you as the world gives. Do not let your hearts be troubled and do not be afraid. (John 14:27) Just so, the Apostle Paul, even while in prison, facing execution, encourages us, "The Lord is near. Do not be anxious about anything, but, in every situation, by prayer and petition, with thanksgiving, present your requests to God. And the peace of God, which transcends all understanding, will guard your hearts and your minds in Christ Jesus." (Philippians 4:5b-7) When the resurrection of Jesus becomes real in our hearts, we, too, can find the peace that passes understanding.

LIFE APPLICATIONS:

1. Describe the things that make you the most anxious. What is it about these things that cause you anxiety, worry or fear?

_____

_____

_____

_____

_____

_____

_____

_____

_____

_____

2. Have you ever sensed his presence, his peace, in times of trouble? Think of some specific examples.

_____

_____

_____

_____

_____

_____

_____

_____

_____

_____

3. Describe your impression of the resurrection in your own terms. What does it mean to you personally? Does it comfort you? If so, how? If not, why not?

_____

_____

_____

_____

_____

_____

_____

_____

_____

_____

4. What does "the peace of Christ" mean to you practically? How do you access it in your life?

_____

_____

_____

_____

_____

_____

_____

_____

_____

_____

39

WAIT FOR ME

Luke 24:44-49

He said to them, "This is what I told you while I was still with you: Everything must be fulfilled that is written about me in the Law of Moses, the Prophets and the Psalms."

Then, he opened their minds so they could understand the Scriptures. He told them, "This is what is written: The Messiah will suffer and rise from the dead on the third day, and repentance for the forgiveness of sins will be preached in his name to all nations, beginning at Jerusalem. You are witnesses of these things. I am going to send you what my Father has promised; but stay in the city until you have been clothed with power from on high." NIV

I CAN'T WAIT

Almost everyone is waiting for something: Waiting for a promotion, waiting for a wedding, or the offer of a wedding ring, waiting to grow up, waiting for a movie release, waiting to own a home, waiting to find happiness. Waiting is a constant condition of life. "I can't wait," is a common exclamation. It's usually hyperbole. We might say it truly of a patient waiting for a heart transplant who will die within days if he doesn't get one, but that's not what we mean by it, generally. "I can't wait," is just a way of saying, "I am so excited about this that waiting is going to be tough."

Right now, I am expecting a couple of books to show up at my door. I ordered them a few days ago, and, since they are from an author I really respect, my anticipation is growing by the day. I can see that the money for the books has come out of my bank account. I have a receipt and a confirmation number that my order has been placed. The seller has sent an email, confirming that my books have been shipped. I know that they'll be here soon—I can't wait!

This dynamic is not a lot different from what the disciples experience between Jesus' resurrection appearance and receiving the Holy Spirit, which Jesus promised them. Jesus forbids them to launch into public action until the Spirit comes. I would imagine, however, that the disciples' waiting operated on a radically higher level than our daily anticipations.

WAIT IN JERUSALEM

Jesus told his disciples, "Behold, I send the promise of my Father upon you; but *tarry* in the city of Jerusalem until you are endued with power from on high." The word, *tarry,* is a highly technical academic term for... okay... maybe just an old word for... ....wait. Jesus told his disciples to wait in Jerusalem until he sends the Holy Spirit to them. That must have been hard... and not a little confusing.

Their encounter with the resurrected Christ had transformed their entire perspective of the world; their lives took on a whole new meaning, and death became little more than the hope of transformation into the full likeness of Jesus in resurrection glory, the putting off of weakness and of temptation and the putting on of eternal, incorruptible power. They didn't just believe it; they, having encountered it, knew it to be true. Yet, Jesus said, *Wait until you are endued with power from on high in the coming of the Spirit.*

They spend "forty days" having Jesus appear to them, teaching them, speaking of the matters of the Kingdom of God. (Acts 1:3) Even on the day of his appearing in that room, where they had stashed themselves away in fear, hiding from the authorities, Jesus opens the Scriptures to them. He reminds their newly enlightened minds of all that he taught while among them, concerning the Law and the Prophets and the Psalms. He reveals himself and his work to them in those pages. Luke says, "And he opened their understanding, that they might comprehend the Scriptures." (Luke 24:44-45) Yet, Jesus said, *Wait until you are endued with power from on high in the coming of the Spirit.*

They go to Jerusalem, like he says, and *they just can't wait.* Their excitement is palpable. We read texts, like Luke 24:52-53, saying, "And they worshiped him and returned to Jerusalem with great joy, and were continually in the temple blessing God." They are emboldened with joy, marching back to Jerusalem after their time with Jesus. Stripped of fear, they go boldly into the temple, blessing God, unintimidated by the authorities there, enriched in knowledge, commissioned by Christ, waiting... waiting.... waiting... Jesus said, *Wait until you are endued with power from on high in the coming of the Spirit.*

Enlightenment, boldness, conviction and knowledge were not enough... they needed to trust Jesus, submit to his wisdom, and wait for his timing. They still needed the empowerment of the Holy Spirit and the divine participation that the Spirit brings to every genuine Christian endeavor.

GOD IS FAITHFUL

God is faithful to his word. If he said it, it will come to pass. We only need to wait for him in faith and trust that, in due time, what he said, he will do. The Lord has always kept his word to me, though I often had to wait for it. This devotional you are reading and the songs of the musical, SAVIOR, that you hear, are all a testimony to God's faithfulness. This SAVIOR project has been years in the making, years in the waiting, and, though I continue to wait on him, God has been faithful to complete the work he's assigned me, to fulfill his call, and to carry out his plan and purpose for my life.

Patient waiting requires trust and not a little confidence in the Lord. If you are struggling with this, remember these words from that death row inmate, Paul, who had every reason to give up on the promises of God, "Being confident of this very thing, that he who has begun a good work in you will complete it until the day of Jesus

Christ." (Philippians 1:6) Hebrews 10:23 echoes his sentiments, "Let us hold fast the confession of our hope without wavering, for he who promised is faithful."

Patient waiting means that we do not get ahead of the Holy Spirit. He is meant to guide us; we are not meant to lead him. The Holy Spirit empowers all we do in the name of Christ. Trust in him; be confident in his Word; wait on his promises; receive his Holy Spirit, knowing that, "Those who wait on the LORD shall renew their strength; they shall mount up with wings like eagles, they shall run and not be weary, they shall walk and not faint." (Isaiah 40:31)

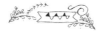

LIFE APPLICATIONS:

1. Do you have a sense of the power and guidance of the Holy Spirit in your life? If so, describe it. If not, why do you think this is? Have you ever sought it in prayer?

_____

_____

_____

_____

_____

_____

_____

_____

_____

2. Does the idea that God has promised to do wonderful things in you and through you for his kingdom ever leave you with a sense of excitement? Explain.

_____

_____

_____

_____

_____

_____

_____

_____

_____

3. In what ways has the Lord come through for you? Are there promises that you feel God has given you that you are still waiting to see come to pass? How are you doing with the waiting process?

_____

_____

_____

_____

_____

_____

_____

_____

_____

_____

40

HE IS RISEN

Matthew 28:16-20

Then the eleven disciples went away into Galilee, to the mountain which Jesus had appointed for them. When they saw Him, they worshiped Him; but some doubted.

And Jesus came and spoke to them, saying, "All authority has been given to Me in heaven and on earth. Go therefore and make disciples of all the nations, baptizing them in the name of the Father and of the Son and of the Holy Spirit, teaching them to observe all things that I have commanded you; and lo, I am with you always, *even* to the end of the age." Amen.

THE GREAT COMMISSION

When Jesus first encountered his disciples three years earlier, they were fishermen, junior varsity types, some were tax collectors, others blue collar roughnecks, not religious leaders and, certainly not, good-Christian boys. They were nobodies. Jesus called them to follow him, setting the groundwork for their relationship, promising to make them fishers of men. They began by watching him, observing how he ministered to the sick, the religious, the poor, the children, the huddled masses. They received special private instruction and mentorship. Then, came their chance. They participated in ever greater ways in his work, following his example and submitting to his critiques. They watched as Jesus did. Then they helped as Jesus did. Then he sent them out... they did as Jesus watched.

Here, in Matthew 28, their time has come. Jesus, though he will always be with them in spirit, intends to leave the work of the Kingdom in their Holy Spirit empowered hands. He, as the resurrected Christ, has received from the Father all authority over heaven and earth.... "that all peoples, nations, and languages should serve him."(Daniel 7:14)

Matthew ends his gospel with what is commonly called The Great Commission, a commission that flows naturally from this authoritative position. Commission, here, is best understood as a mission given by one and received by another. Consider it Jesus' charter for his Church. It is the Christian's purpose statement. It's your mission, if you choose to receive it, if you regard yourself as Jesus' disciple—to go and make disciples.

A DISCIPLE MAKING DISCIPLES

I believe that there is a difference between a believer and a disciple. The day I opened my heart to Christ, I became a believer; I knew Christ had died for me, had forgiven me of my sins, and had called me into a relationship with him. I determined that I was going to follow, but becoming a disciple, as I understand the term, would take time and discipline.

My friends, David and his wife, Shelby, were instrumental in my own discipleship. We'd have Bible studies at their house; they'd answer my unending questions and pray for me. They were there for me in my life, helping me and loving me, even when I faced difficulty putting the Scriptures into practice. It was hard work, at times, but it was beautiful all the same. I have a great love and appreciation for them putting up with me while my weak faith became strong, and I eventually began discipling others.

These days, I am the worship and arts director and small groups pastor at my church. In the mission of the small groups ministry, I ask my leaders to teach a weekly group, to meet with the other small group leaders once a month and to mentor someone in their group regularly, one-on-one. I use the term mentor because that's discipleship in a nutshell. It's as the Apostle Paul states, "Follow my example as I follow the example of Christ." (1 Corinthians 11:1 NIV) This commitment starts with the discipler. Disciple making requires rolling up our sleeves and getting our hands dirty. It demands involvement in the messy lives of others. It is time consuming, and inconvenient, and exhausting and is one of the best things you can ever do with your life.

MAKING DISCIPLE MAKERS

Today, the word Christian can take on different meanings. Jesus, however, never called his followers Christians, he called them disciples. The term disciple, though seldom used today, is far more accurate. Perhaps, the similarity of the terms (disciple & discipline) has already struck you. Whatever else we do as Christians, the most basic instructions given to us in this final great commission of Jesus is to lead others into the discipline of Christ. We are called to be disciples, making disciples who make disciples—so we are disciples making disciple makers. This is so much more than periodically preaching at people, or sharing the gospel with them and, then, leaving them to work it all out on their own. I imagine this process in terms of raising and nourishing a child. If, according to John 3:7, becoming a true believer in Christ means being "born again," we might easily imagine the new Christian in terms of a spiritual child that needs teaching, training, love and discipline in order to develop into a mature disciple.

Three elements in this commission scream "THIS IS SERIOUS BUSINESS!!!"

The first element of seriousness is the scale of the commission. In a nation viciously self-involved and full of contempt for outsiders, Jesus calls for his disciples to make disciples of *all* nations—it's global. It involves every culture, every language, every place where people have gone in every part of the world… excluding none, hunting them all out to win them to Christ, or to die trying.

The second element of the seriousness of this commission is the sealing of discipleship with baptism. Baptism was how people committed themselves to a particular person or community in Jesus' day; it was like signing a legal document with God as witness. Its very symbolism was cleansing and death—Jesus' death, the disciple's invitation of death for unfaithfulness, and the disciple's death to his or her old way of life.

The third element of the seriousness of the commission is its content—OBEDIENCE. Some people forget that Christ actually gave us commandments. Commands just seem so Old Testament and out of sorts with the more hip, friendly, suggestive Jesus of the New Testament. To many, Jesus is all "sheep snuggling" and "baby kissing" without all the demands and discipline of religious "sticks-in-the-mud." Christ gave many commands recorded in the gospels, and defended the whole of Scripture as divine word. As challenging as interpretation can be, we are called to teach obedience to all of it.

BE A DISCIPLE MAKING DISCIPLES

Jesus' commission to the eleven on that mountain two thousand years ago is a commission to you and me as well. If you've committed your life to the SAVIOR, that chain of disciples making disciple-making disciples leads straight to your door. You are a part of this; you belong to a great cause; you have a purpose; your purpose is not merely going to church, building up a nest egg, keeping yourself entertained, while trying to be good until you die and go to Heaven. This call, this commission, comes to you and it comes to me—"Go and make disciples of all nations, baptizing them in the name of the Father and of the Son and of the Holy Spirit, and teaching them to obey everything I have commanded you." The Great Commission isn't "Go to church"; it's "Be the Church"... by going into all the world, making disciples. The world is lost in darkness; we are called to be lights. Can there be a more noble calling? A more important cause? A greater investment of our life? Not in my accounting, no. There can be no greater cause, no greater return on our investment than to bring souls, to bring disciple-making disciples into the kingdom of heaven. Go, therefore...

LIFE APPLICATIONS:

1. Describe in your own words the Great Commission. Describe what it means to be a disciple of Jesus. Would you consider yourself a disciple? Do you feel that you have been discipled by others in the Church?

_____

_____

_____

_____

_____

_____

_____

_____

2. Do you feel that you belong to the church and its mission of making disciple makers? Have you ever sought to win people to Christ? Have you ever sought to disciple others? If not, why not?

_____

_____

_____

_____

_____

_____

_____

_____

3. Do you feel compelled to study Scripture in order to know and obey the commands of God and Christ? Describe your relationship to Scripture.

_____

_____

_____

_____

_____

_____

_____

_____

_____

4. Describe your beliefs about Jesus. (Compare your answer with the first answer you gave in chapter 1. If they've changed, explain how.)

_____

_____

_____

_____

_____

_____

_____

_____

_____

CONCLUSION

Congratulations on completing this part of your life-long journey with the SAVIOR! We hope that this devotional has been a blessing to you, helping you in your spiritual walk. It is through much prayer and hard work that you hear the songs of SAVIOR, hold this book in your hands (or read it on your screen). I, along with many others, have prayed that your life would be richly rewarded by the experience.

It has been our intention in writing this that you would encounter Jesus the SAVIOR in a new and vital way, that you would become an empowered disciple of Christ, and vastly expand your sense of connection to the longstanding community of those who have devoted everything to the Son of God, sharing, as you do, so many of the same struggles in faith and devotion. Our hope for you now is that your relationship with him would be strengthened and that you will continue to grow by what you have heard and what you have learned. Be both a disciple and a disciple-maker

If you have never fully committed your life to Christ, I would like to offer this moment to you now, here at the end of this journey, to make that commitment, to surrender your will to his, to repent of your sins and to follow his plan and purpose for your life.

I would like to offer you this prayer for your own use as a help and a guide in your pursuit of Salvation through faith in Jesus Christ.

> "Lord Jesus, I recognize that I am a sinner who has
> lived in rebellion against you, please forgive my sins,
> cleanse me from all unrighteousness, help me to
> overcome my struggles with sin going forward. I
> believe that you came, died and rose again for me and
> that my life has no greater purpose than to be lived
> fulfilling your will for me and for this world. Help me
> become your committed disciple, learning and

obeying your word in the Scriptures, that I might
fulfill your Great Commission to be a disciple-maker.
Empower me by your Holy Spirit to become more
and more like you. Amen."

If you've made a commitment to Christ, you don't want to walk
the rest of your journey alone. Find a Bible believing church that
contains a group of disciples that will help you grow in your own
journey with the SAVIOR. Introduce yourself to the pastor(s) and get
involved with the small group studies they may have there. If you
already have a church, get busy making disciple making disciples.

I would like to conclude this devotional by praying for you.

*"Father, I pray that you would bless all those who have
diligently applied themselves to hearing from you in the course of
this devotional. Jesus, as the seed planted in good ground begins
to take root and grow, may your Word find good soil and may
the seed of your Word grow and flourish in the heart and minds
of all who have gone through this devotional journey. May we be
made your disciples as your Word and the lessons in this book
are applied to our everyday lives and may our faith increase in
the days ahead. Holy Spirit, help us to make disciples and help
us all to know you more and know that you are with us,
leading us and guiding us—even till the end of the age. In
Jesus' name, I pray, amen"*

END NOTES

[i] There were boxes containing particular texts of Scripture that were strapped onto the head and hands. The laws governing the wearing of phylacteries were derived by the Rabbis from four Biblical passages (Deut. vi. 8, xi. 18; Ex. xiii. 9, 16). http://www.jewishencyclopedia.com/articles/12125-phylacteries. (2/6/2013).

[ii] Andrew Sargent, "Jesus had an Identity Crisis: Christ & Son of God in Mark 1:1. http://drandrewsargent.com/2014/01/jesus-had-an-identity-crisis-christ-son-of-god-in-mark-11/

[iii] Barnes, 652.

[iv] You may want to read the book *The Case for Christ, by Lee Strobel.*

[v] Barnes, 444.

[vi] F.C Cook, M.A., The Holy Bible Commentary and a Revision of the Translation by Bishops and Other Clergy of the Anglican Church, (New York: Charles Scribner's and Sons), 178.

[vii] Law, 172.

[viii] Aleister Crowley & the Abby of Thelma ttp://www.thelema101.com/intro 6/24/2014

[ix] William Law, *A Serious Call to a Devout and Holy Life*, pg. 70.

[x] This is my favorite gag from James Dobson's *Life on the Edge*, (Nashville: Word Publishing, 1995).

[xi] Some suggest that his resurrection body left him unrecognizable to their mortal eyes.

[xii] Thank You, dear Gary Larson, *Far Side* creator; My dog's name is Roadie.

Made in the USA
Columbia, SC
01 April 2019